KT-560-068

Practical
Pre-School

What Learning Looks Like...

Mathematical Development

Caroline Jones

Contents

About this book

This book takes a close look at the area of learning which is concerned with children's mathematical development. In England and Wales this is called Mathematical Development; in Northern Ireland, Early Mathematical Experiences; and in Scotland it forms part of Knowledge and Understanding of the World.

Guidance and good practice

The author explains what the area of learning consists of, what the jargon means and how it applies to the various settings in the Foundation Stage of education - children aged between three and rising six.

There are four different curriculum bodies across the United Kingdom - the Qualifications and Curriculum Authority (QCA) in England; the Curriculum and Assessment Authority for Wales (Awdurdod Cwricwlwm Ac Asesu Cymru); the Scottish Consultative Council on the Curriculum; and the Northern Ireland Council for the Curriculum Examinations and Assessment. Each has a different statement relating to the desired curriculum for young children. However, although there are some differences in terminology and some slight variations in emphasis, good practice in one country is still considered good practice in another.

As well as giving theoretical guidance - albeit in practical terms - the book also aims to give an outline of activities which can be used to deliver the curriculum requirements.

Practical activities

All these activities should be considered as merging into the normal life of the early years setting. The book stresses the importance of play and how the areas of learning are linked. The activities are not prescriptive and should not be seen as tasks to complete. They are designed to be manageable and fun.

There are suggestions for 15 activities. Some are simple and straightforward activities which need few resources. Others are deliberately more challenging. Each can be used in some form with children at different stages of development.

The activities are planned to cover all aspects of mathematics in the early years. Each one focuses on a specific Early Learning Goal (ELG) but since these overlap and interrelate with one another the activities, therefore, often fulfil more than one goal.

All children develop at different rates. Children within the Foundation Stage move along a continuum and their progress will not necessarily be steady or uniform. Although some reference is made to younger and older children, the activities suggested are all designed to cover a range of levels of understanding. Activities must not be thought of as age appropriate but developmentally appropriate. Within your group you will have children who are at different stages of development. You should adapt and change the ideas to make them more appropriate for the needs of individual children. The activities are only ideas and should not be seen as prescriptive models!

Planning

A planning chart has been included for support and guidance but we would encourage you to adapt this readily to meet your own needs and circumstances.

There are seven books in this series, and although each book can be used by itself, they are designed to fit together so that the whole learning framework is covered.

The seven titles are:

❑ Personal, Social and Emotional Development

❑ Communication, Language and Literacy

❑ Mathematical Development

❑ Knowledge and Understanding of the World: Geography and History

❑ Knowledge and Understanding of the World: Science and Technology

❑ Physical Development

❑ Creative Development

All of these books carry some activities based on common themes which, when used together, will give enough ideas for a cross-curricular topic over a half or even a full term.

The common themes are:

❑ Seasons

❑ Water

❑ Colour

❑ All about me

❑ People who help us

All the books together provide an outline of the learning which should be taking place in the Foundation Stage.

Assessment

Each activity includes suggestions for assessment. Assessment involves two distinct activities:

❑ The gathering of information about the child's capabilities.

❑ Making a judgement based on this information.

Assessment should not take place in isolation. We assess to meet individual needs and ensure progress. The following ideas may help your assessment to be more effective.

❑ Assessment is a continuous process. It should be systematic to ensure all children are observed on a regular basis.

❑ Assessment should always start with the child. The first steps in providing appropriate provision is by sensitively observing children to identify their learning needs.

❑ Assessment should not take place to see how much the child has learned but should take place to plan appropriately for future activities.

❑ You should be a participant in the assessment process, interacting and communicating with the child.

The main way of assessing the young child is through careful observation.

Observations should:

❑ Record both the positive and negative behaviour shown.

❑ Be long enough to make the child's behaviour meaningful.

❑ Record only what you see and not what you think you have seen or heard.

❑ Be clear - before you begin be sure you know what you want to observe.

❑ Be organised - plan ahead, otherwise it will not happen.

National guidelines

In spite of the variations between the frameworks in Northern Ireland, England, Scotland and Wales, there is a common message. All young children are entitled to a range of well-planned, good quality, practical, enjoyable and meaningful mathematical experiences.

The English Early Learning Goals

The *Curriculum Guidance for the Foundation Stage* is organised into six areas of learning. These explain the knowledge, skills and understanding that most children will be expected to achieve by the end of the Foundation Stage and consist of Personal, Social and Emotional Development, Communication, Language and Literacy, Mathematical Development, Knowledge and Understanding of the World, Creative Development and Physical Development.

Early Learning Goals (ELGs) are broken down into learning activities for children at various stages of development. These are called stepping stones and should be used in planning to help children achieve the ELGs.

The Foundation Stage runs from the age of three to the end of the Reception year. In England, children start school at various ages depending on where they live. In some areas, for example, children start full-time education in the September following their fourth birthday, whereas elsewhere they may not be admitted until the term in which they are five.

Assessing whether a child has achieved the goals needs to take into account the child's age at the end of the Reception year.

It is important to note that the goals are not viewed as one-off achievements which can be 'taught' at a particular point in time. Rather, they are expressions of intended outcomes at the end of the Foundation Stage. Logically, children in pre-school settings would not normally be expected to achieve the goals before they start school. Instead, the pre-school setting and indeed the Reception class teacher should be providing activities and experiences which are likely to ensure that in the longer term - ie at the end of the Foundation Stage - most children will attain the goals.

The Early Learning Goals appear straightforward. However, they represent the outcome or end product of a complex teaching and learning process. In the area of Mathematical Development there are 12 goals or objectives, although some can be further sub-divided. These correspond to the key objectives in the *National numeracy strategy; Framework for teaching for the Reception year*. They fall into three broad categories:

❑ Numbers as labels and for counting
❑ Calculating
❑ Shape, space and measures

The first group begins with the expectation that children will be able to say and use number names in order in familiar contexts. This aspect also

includes counting reliably up to ten everyday objects and recognising numerals one to nine.

The second area, calculating, is all about using numbers in practical situations, for example laying a table for four people or sharing six sweets between three children and being able to talk about numbers in everyday life.

The third group relates to children talking about a range of mathematical ideas. By the end of the Foundation Stage they should be able to recognise and talk about shape, size, patterns and position using appropriate language. They should learn the language of comparison:

❑ 'use language such as 'greater', 'smaller', 'heavier' or 'lighter' to compare quantities.'

And be able to talk about the properties of different shapes:

❑ 'use language such as 'circle' or 'bigger' to describe the shape and size of solids and flat shapes.'

Positional words such as 'on', 'above', 'below' and 'under' are not specified but there is an implicit assumption that they will be used as children are expected to:

❑ 'use everyday words to describe position.'

The Early Learning Goals for Mathematical Development provide a structure for planning the educational environment and experiences for children from the age of three. However, it is important to remember that children will experience a wide range of mathematics in the world outside the pre-school or school setting and this will play an important part in achieving the goals.

The Scottish Curriculum Framework

The Scottish *Curriculum Framework for Children 3 to 5* is based on five key aspects of learning and experience. Interestingly, mathematical

development is the one area that is not included as a separate area of learning. Instead, several mathematical elements of learning are incorporated within Knowledge and Understanding of the World. On the one hand, this is positive as it acknowledges that mathematics is an integral part of all the aspects of learning. On the other, for planning purposes at least, it is useful to have mathematical development separated out so that it does not become absorbed elsewhere or given lower priority than it deserves. In being part of Knowledge and Understanding of the World, mathematics is accorded the status of not simply being a basis for later numeracy but valuable in a much wider context. The Scottish framework specifies that children need to recognise colours and places mathematics in the context of the children's lives:

❑ Recognise patterns, shapes and colours in the world around them.

As with the Welsh document, sorting and categorising are given high priority. Measurement is specifically mentioned and in particular the Scottish framework makes explicit reference to children being aware of:

❑ daily time sequences and words to describe and measure time, for example snack time, morning, first, next, clock.

The Scottish guidance encourages the use of mathematical language but emphasises that this must be in appropriate contexts. The word 'play' is not explicitly included in the statements for the English Goals. In the Scottish framework, many of the elements include the word 'play' and refer to real contexts. Examples of this include the expectation that children should learn to:

❏ identify and use numbers up to ten in play situations;

❏ recognise familiar shapes during play activities.

The framework suggests that 'lots of practical experience gives children confidence with number, which helps them when they move to ideas such as 'one more' or 'one less' and to written representations of number'. Reference is also made to larger numbers in the environment such as house numbers or bus numbers. Problem-solving is encouraged as part of children's growing understanding of mathematics.

The Northern Ireland Curricular Guidance for Pre-school Education

The Northern Ireland guidance was published in 1997. It clearly states that there is no place for an established body of knowledge or set of skills to be mastered in pre-school settings. Instead it suggests that the curriculum should evolve from the needs of the child. The Northern Ireland guidance uses the title Early Mathematical Experiences rather than Mathematical Development. It suggests play as an effective way of fostering mathematical concepts and developing positive attitudes to mathematics. Several examples of how children can begin to learn mathematical language and concepts through play are given. For example, children learn about:

❏ space as they build with large blocks on the floor;

❏ size as they order a variety of dolls;

❏ number as they lay a table;

relationships as they pretend to cook and place the correct lids on saucepans.

The Northern Ireland guidance is expressed in child-friendly terminology rather than a list of goals. It is altogether much less prescriptive or rigidly expressed than the Early Learning Goals. It makes reference to rhymes, stories, songs and seasonal events such as birthdays. It clearly links mathematics with role play, physical play, sand, water and so on. A general description is given of the characteristics and skills that the majority of children who have experienced appropriate pre-school education will display in terms of mathematics. It is worth quoting in full:

'Children begin to understand early concepts of size and quantity. They use mathematical language, such as heavy, light, full, empty, short, more, another, big and little in relevant contexts. Through talking about daily routines and seasonal events, and waiting to take turns, they show an awareness of time. They begin to understand and use positional words, such as, in front of, behind above and below. They talk about shapes in their environment.

'Children solve problems as they play, questioning, predicting and experimenting. In the course of their play they sort, match, order, sequence and count. They learn number rhymes and songs, and listen to stories which have an element of mathematics in them.'

Curricular Guidance for Pre-School Education (NICCEA) (page 19)

The Welsh Desirable Outcomes for Children's Learning before Compulsory School Age

The Welsh document is based on the six areas of learning, the third of which is entitled Mathematical Development. The current Welsh guidance is based on three terms of pre-school experience. Consequently it covers intended outcomes for four-year-olds, whereas the English Early Learning Goals include five-year-olds in Reception classes.

In the Welsh document, there is an explicit emphasis on mathematical processes and concepts as the foundation of numeracy and the importance of number concepts being presented in three ways:

❏ visual;

❏ concrete;

❏ practical.

In addition, the guidance explains the need for children to:

❏ see it done;

❏ do it themselves.

There are seven elements within the area of Mathematical Development in the Welsh guidance. Firstly, and in common with the Early Learning Goals, there is an expectation that children will be introduced to mathematical language in relevant contexts: shape, position, size and quantity. This element is more general than that in the Early Learning Goals in that it does not make reference to specific words. The assumption perhaps is that being less prescriptive leaves more discretion to the practitioners. There is, for example, no specific requirement for children to say and use number names or count reliably up to ten everyday objects. Instead, as the Welsh document is aimed at younger children, it suggests that children should:

❑ recall a range of number rhymes, songs, stories and counting games;

❑ sort, match, order, sequence, compare and count familiar objects.

The skill of sorting and classifying has not been explicitly included in the Early Learning Goals, in spite of being an essential prerequisite to many other aspects of mathematical development. Another aspect included in the Welsh document that does not feature overtly in the Early Learning Goals is that children should:

❑ begin to understand the mathematics of money.

This aspect is not included in the English Early Learning Goals, although it is often a common introduction to mathematics outside the nursery or school situation. Indeed, for younger and particularly school age children (and adults!) it is the most useful and common application of mathematics. In role play children learn a great deal of mathematics from playing shops and cafes, as they sort and weigh goods, write price lists, use tills, and so on.

The emphasis is on introducing mathematical concepts to children rather than attaining a definitive outcome at a certain point in time. There is an expectation that in nursery children should:

❑ begin to recognise numbers and begin to match number to sign and sound;

❑ begin to understand mathematical concepts such as 'less' and 'more'.

Undoubtedly, the Welsh guidance is more appropriate for nursery age children whereas the Early Learning Goals are specifically directed towards the end of the Reception year. The Welsh document may actually serve as a useful introductory phase to the Early Learning Goals.

The area of learning explained

Mathematics is everywhere in a child's life. However, the word 'mathematics' conjures up negative associations for many adults. Not surprisingly, perhaps, some early years practitioners may even question the wisdom of 'teaching' mathematics to three-year-olds.

Making maths fun

Maths is associated with rote learning and practice out of context leading to inevitable failure for many. As a result of inappropriate mathematical experiences children can lose confidence and develop low self-esteem. Therefore adults working with young children need to ensure that mathematical learning is grounded in meaningful contexts and presented in appropriate ways, which relate to children's levels of experience and understanding.

'One of the aims of mathematics education in early childhood is for children to see maths as interesting, relevant, enjoyable and worthwhile: finding that numbers can amuse, delight, illuminate and explain.'

(*Te Whariki* The New Zealand Early Childhood Guidelines)

Why teach mathematics?

It is important for the early years worker to consider what is involved in Mathematical Development and the reasons why it is an essential part of the young child's educational programme. It has been suggested that the mathematics teacher has four tasks. (*Mathematics Counts*, 1982) These four

tasks are a useful way of thinking about why mathematical experiences are important in the early years. They are to:

❑ enable each child to develop skills and understanding needed for adult life;

❑ provide the mathematics needed for the study of other subjects;

❑ help each pupil develop appreciation for and enjoyment of mathematics and its importance;

❑ provide a powerful means of communication.

Although mathematics is presented as a list of separate goals in the Early Learning Goals, this separation should be seen as mainly for planning purposes.

In practice, young children do not learn effectively in subject compartments. Learning ranges across the six areas and indeed within the separate elements in Mathematical Development. One area or aspect is frequently supporting, reinforcing and consolidating another. Through one activity children will be learning a range of skills and concepts at the same time. However, some of the Early Learning Goals in mathematics do contain certain concepts that will need to be understood, at least partly, before others can be achieved. An example of this is that children will need to say and use the number names in sequence before they can count a given number of everyday objects. However,

more often than not, children will be learning about a combination of aspects at the same time.

It is important not to underestimate children's capabilities regarding mathematics. Understanding is enhanced by discussion and questions, which challenge children and encourage them to think without feeling under pressure. Activities and questions can be adapted to meet the needs of all children. Although the goals are expressed in terms of outcomes for the end of the reception year, it is important to note that it is the processes that are important, rather than the outcomes.

The Early Learning Goals – a closer look

These are the intended goals for children at the end of their Reception year. In other words, they explain what most children are expected to achieve after six terms of frequent mathematical experiences. The key point is that the goals are not something that can be achieved or taught overnight. Mathematical knowledge, skills and understanding are acquired through a gradual process, experienced over a long period of time.

Adults need to plan the children's experiences through play and practical activities that will give the children a foundation to build up their knowledge, skills and understanding. Children will return and revisit all the aspects in order to apply and consolidate what they have learned in different contexts. Maths is everywhere and mathematical development, including numeracy, depends on becoming confident and competent during the Foundation Stage.

What is important is that a particular activity meets each child's individual learning needs. In number rhymes, for example, a three-year-old may simply be encouraged to use those which involve numbers one to five, whereas a four-year-old may manage to ten. Older nursery and Reception children may also begin to count back, using rhymes such as 'Ten green bottles' or 'Five little monkeys'. The adult questioning or amount of adult support needed to complete a task can be adapted according to the child's level of understanding.

Moving children towards these goals can be achieved through many everyday activities in nursery or pre-school settings and in Reception classes. Some activities will need to be planned and focussed, others will occur spontaneously in children's daily lives at home and at school. Many will happen or can be planned as part of the daily routine, for example, counting the number of children present or learning to sort and classify as they tidy away toys and equipment. Good planning will lead to progression as children learn and develop.

Mathematical understanding can and should be developed through practical experiences, underpinned by oral development. These would include number rhymes, counting and matching games, stories, baking, construction play, sand and water play and imaginative play. Activities should be enjoyable and imaginative.

The first three Early Learning Goals in Mathematical Development are related to recognising and using number names in real contexts.

Saying and using number names

Number rhymes are an excellent way to introduce children to number names and should be a regular part of a young child's routine. Children can participate in action rhymes, for example 'Peter hammers with one hammer' or 'Five fat sausages', and hold up the appropriate number of fingers. They can take turns to be the five currant buns or five little monkeys jumping on the bed! They can help make visual aids such as paper plates on lollipop sticks that become five little ducks or speckled frogs. Commercial resources, such as finger puppets or

interactive Velcro-board versions of popular rhymes are available. Other popular rhymes are 'Five stripy socks' and 'Five little peas in a pea pod pressed'. Popular number rhyme tapes and storybooks are also available to help children say and use names in order. It is useful to have a list of number rhymes available for quick reference.

Once they know some of the names the children will begin to transfer that knowledge to spontaneous use of numbers in familiar contexts. Even before they can count reliably, children will begin to experiment using the names of numbers. In the role-play area, for example, they may count out the money or whilst playing with bricks they may say 'Look! I've got four'. Outside they might count how many hops or jumps they do or say the number names as they climb the steps on the slide. At first they may not say the names in order, but this will come with encouragement and practice. Children may also say and use the names of larger numbers that have meaning to them as individuals, even though they cannot actually count that far. These may include house numbers and bus numbers or the ages of friends and family members. Children's birthdays also provide another opportunity to use number names in a meaningful and familiar context: 'I'm three', 'My brother is 16', and 'It's my dad's birthday - he's 21!' Children need to be comfortably familiar with number names in order to help them count reliably.

I can count!

Children need to have a purpose for counting. It must be meaningful for them. The key is to use familiar everyday objects. Many opportunities will arise as part of children's normal routines. In pre-school settings, for example, encourage children to count how many cups are needed for the table at snack time or how many biscuits. For older children, organise resources in pots with labelled numbers. They then count the resources as they put them away, for example, ten paintbrushes in the paintbrush holder, six pairs of scissors per pot. In planned activities, such as baking cakes, encourage children to join in counting the number of eggs

used or spoonfuls of flour.

In the early stages, children have a tendency to go too fast and to lose the sequence. It is not uncommon to hear 'one, two, three, four, five' and then 'eight, eleven, ten, twelve'. It is important that you observe this and note where the child is having difficulty. Once they reach the threshold of understanding they may just say any number or even make a number name up, such as 'twenteen'. They know some number names but have not yet achieved the idea of one-to-one correspondence - that one number equals one object.

Encourage children to touch the objects as they count. Children show an understanding of counting when they are able to say how many there are in a given group of objects or people. For example, if you ask, 'How many are there?' and the child gives the correct number of objects, or if you say, 'Pass me three bricks, please' and the child

gives the right number.

Although children do need to practise it is important not to become carried away with asking them to count anything and everything that moves. Far better to build constantly on spontaneous opportunities arising in play and in the daily routine.

Recognising numbers

Children need to be encouraged to recognise numerals 1 to 9 during the Foundation Stage. However, the actual numeral, which represents a given number of objects, is an abstract concept for a young child. They can be helped to recognise numbers as representations of a quantity of objects through a number rich environment. Number charts, height charts and number tiles and friezes that show pictorial groups and numerals should be displayed at child height. If, for example, a number chart is near where the children line up to go outside or to the toilet, they can look at the number chart while they are waiting. Encourage children to use the charts independently. If a child in Reception class asks 'What's a five?' she could be directed or taken to the number chart to see if she can find it for herself. Children could be involved in creating class number charts, lines or ladders. Outdoors there could be a number snake for the children to hop and jump along.

Children enjoy activities such as building towers on clearly written numeral cards. They could be challenged to put the correct numbers of bricks or cubes on the appropriate numeral card. This also shows how the tower increases in height as the number becomes bigger. Similarly, toy cars, farm animals, buttons, shells, conkers and so on could be used to make sets that match the numeral.

Children can then move on to match pictorial sets to numerals. They can

consolidate their learning through small group activities such as completing number jigsaw puzzles or playing number games which require them to match numeral to set, such as snap or dominoes. Older children could make their own books for each number - cutting out pictures from magazines or catalogues and sticking the corresponding number on each page.

Reinforce and share learning with parents by having a number of the week. Each day at register time choose a child. Show the numeral to the child who picks out the number of objects to match the number of the week.

A number washing line can be a source of interactive activities and helps children to order numbers. Point to each number and count together along the line. You could pretend to play a trick and put a number in the wrong place, then choose a child to come and put it into the right place each day, gradually making it more difficult. More and more numbers can be used as children become more adept at recognising and ordering numbers.

You can also make the most of numbers in the environment, pointing out when they appear on signposts, children's clothing labels, birthday cards, dates and recipes. Popular dice games such as Incy Wincy Spider and Giant Snakes and Ladders are another good resource for helping children recognise numerals in a practical and enjoyable way. Other resources such as calculators, tills, toy money, price lists, telephones, catalogues and telephone directories in the role-play area will also encourage children to recognise the numerals in their play.

Let's talk maths!

Encourage children to use mathematical language to compare either numbers in a set or quantities of particular substances such as sand and water. Words such as 'more' or 'less',

'greater' or 'smaller', 'heavier' or 'lighter', should be used regularly by adults and children alike. Extend mathematical vocabulary, for example, through sand and water tray activities, an essential part of every child's early mathematical experiences. Straw, rice, sawdust, soil, pasta and tea leaves make interesting alternatives. They are invaluable for comparison of quantities.

An important part of this aspect of mathematics is that children should be exploring and experimenting. They need opportunities to compare quantities as they use a variety of funnels, plastic bottles, teapots, cups and containers of various shapes and sizes. It is up to you to then encourage the use of mathematical language. Effective questioning allows children to develop their understanding in a meaningful context. Key questions such as 'Which holds the most?' and 'How many egg cups of rice do you think you will need to fill that pot?' can be displayed by the sand tray as a reminder.

Activities such as pouring coloured water or sand through sieves and funnels also develop children's understanding of capacity. Children could collect plastic containers from home, such as sauce, pop or water bottles, yoghurt pots and margarine containers. Introduce older children to litre and half-litre containers. Baking is another regular activity that encourages children to think about quantities and helps to set the mathematical language into context. It can also be useful for introducing concepts such as 'heavy' and 'light'. Allow children to play with scales to explore the idea of balance. You could start with obvious things such as a feather and a stone. Again, use questioning to introduce the vocabulary and to encourage children to respond using the same words.

Mathematical language should also be used to help children compare numbers in a set. Encourage them to think, to estimate and to compare groups of objects. Ask the children questions and use the language so that it becomes a familiar part of their vocabulary. 'Are there more cars in this garage or that garage?' 'Which bus has more passengers?' 'Which train has more carriages?' 'Which one has the smallest number of carriages?' Children adept at counting can check if they are right. 'Johnny has some red teddies. Jane has blue ones. How many have you got?' 'Who has the most?'

To add or to take away?

Apart from using mathematical language to compare numbers or quantity children should begin to use the vocabulary involved in adding and subtracting. In practical activities and discussion they will use various words to talk about addition and subtraction. These include 'altogether', 'more than' and 'less than'. Children need to understand that the language of addition involves combining two numbers or groups of objects. Again, it is important to use everyday situations. At snack time, for example, you might put two biscuits on a plate when there are six children at the table. You could then ask questions such as: 'How many do we need altogether?' 'So how many more biscuits do we need?' 'If I take one away, how many are left?' It is the adult modelling and use of the language associated with addition and subtraction that will encourage the child to use mathematical vocabulary. Words like 'take away', 'add' and 'subtract' will become part of a child's everyday vocabulary if used often enough in practical situations. Activities such as role play and cooking also provide ideal opportunities for children to practise what they have learned.

Children learn through solving simple problems and should be frequently asked the question 'How many more?'. 'There are two people in the role-play area, four are allowed, so how many more can go in?' Similarly, with subtraction, words such as 'take away' or 'less' come into play situations. Small group activities using everyday objects such as toy cars, counters, cubes, bricks or shells can also be used to practise and assess children's level of understanding.

At first, children will be able to combine two groups of objects and work out the total or take some objects away and count the number left. Eventually they will be able to add or subtract one or two from a given number. As they develop confidence and understanding they will know number bonds, such as two and two make four, and begin to use bigger numbers. Tackling sheets of written sums at this stage is not appropriate. There is little point in using the written symbols until the child is able to apply the number operation correctly. Children should be allowed to develop their own ways of adding and subtracting.

Eventually they will be able to apply this knowledge and use the language in simple calculations. To begin with they should be encouraged to find one more or one less than a number to ten.

Before children can achieve this element they need to be competent in counting both backwards and forwards to ten. Number rhymes are useful in this area, for example, 'Five little speckled frogs' - There were five frogs, one jumped into the pool, how many are left? 'Five little ducks' and 'Ten green bottles' serve a similar purpose. A small group activity such as building a tower of up to ten bricks then taking one off and asking the child to predict and then count how many are left will help them work towards this element. You should make the most of opportunities during play to take one away or add one on. This can then be extended to early addition and subtraction.

Early addition relates to combining two groups of objects. Conversely, subtraction is related to 'taking away' one or more objects from a group of objects.

At first, children need experiences in seeing and dividing numbers of objects into two different groups, for example different coloured cubes or bricks. If you arrange ten cubes, including two green and three blue ones, in one group and then children divide them by colour, you could ask 'How many blue cubes?', 'How many green cubes?', 'How many altogether?' Coloured sweets such as Smarties or jelly babies can make this a popular activity. Subtract one as they eat one! The first step is to make sure that children see the relationship between the various numbers of objects in the set.

Let's make a pattern!

Mathematics is permeated by patterns. As they recognise, create or copy patterns children will become aware that some relationships are consistent and can be predicted and recreated. There are a number of ways in which patterns can be presented to children. They could be introduced to the idea by looking at patterns around them, such as on wallpaper, materials and clothing. Tea towels, jumpers and wrapping paper are all good resources for this topic. Outside, encourage children to look for patterns in brickwork, tiles, paving slabs and zebra crossings. Clapping patterns in music or looking at pictures of tigers, butterflies and zebras will extend children's experience in this area. You should make explicit reference to the repetitive nature of the pattern.

Children can be encouraged to copy patterns through activities such as bead threading, peg boards and Duplo bricks. Various commercial resources such as Linking Elephants and Compare Bears include pre-prepared cards that encourage pattern making in increasing levels of difficulty. A number of excellent computer programs are also available in this area. Ultimately, children should recognise a pattern and be able to continue it by predicting what comes next. At first this may involve patterns with colours, sizes, numbers or shapes. Later, children may begin to use numbers. When children are seen spontaneously making their own patterns you will know that they have grasped the concept.

A square or a cube?

Shape is a common topic in most early years settings. The children need to be able to sort and classify shapes into sets before formally naming them. 'Can you find one like this?' 'Yes, it's a circle isn't it?' 'Can you find another circle?' Ask questions about the property of the shape. 'How many corners has it got?' 'How many straight edges?' Shapes can be incorporated into the environment, for example using posters and painted shapes outdoors or on the hall floor. Children can learn to recognise and name shapes as they play games such as shape lotto, shape dominoes or match a shape. Activities such as 'guess the shape' using a feely

bag or 'hunt the shape' are also fun. It is important to use the correct shape names and to include solid shapes. A 'shape table' might include a collection of boxes, balls and wheels. Encourage children to recognise shapes in the environment such as carpet tiles, wheels, windows, doors and tables.

Under or over?

It is important for adults to model positional language for children, to ask questions during play and to play games with the children using positional language. Children need to understand words describing position in order to progress in their mathematical problem-solving and thinking. Often adults assume that children understand what phrases such as 'in front of' or 'next to' mean. A blank face on a child who has been asked to 'Stand in front of Michael' may indicate otherwise. Words such as 'before' and 'after' are used in questions such as 'What number comes after five?' but if the child does not understand the meaning of 'comes after' she will not be able to answer the question. Introduce other positions such as 'behind' and 'on top of' in everyday situations; in construction play, for example, by asking a child to put another brick 'on top of' the tower. 'Above' and 'below', 'up' and 'down', 'beside', 'under' and 'over' are further examples. Outdoor play, physical development and obstacle courses also offer ideal opportunities for promoting positional language.

No problem!

'The ability to solve problems is at the heart of mathematics' (*Mathematics Counts*, 1982 para 249). Children need opportunities to solve simple number related problems. If there are four children in the role-play area, for example, they should be encouraged to set the table for the right number of people. Children should encounter

problems relating to sharing - 'If we (four children) have eight biscuits, how many can we have each?' 'How can we make the scales balance?' 'How many sandwiches do we need?' Children should also be given opportunities to solve problems involving sorting, classifying and matching as well as in sand, water and construction play. 'How can we make this tower smaller/taller/the same as this one?' Problem-solving allows children to think mathematically and to make decisions in order to find solutions.

Approaching teaching and learning

As with any area of learning, the teaching of mathematics requires a variety of approaches. Mathematics needs to be presented in a variety of ways. How teaching and learning is organised will depend on the nature of the activity, the number of children and the number of adults. The adult role is crucial and it is important that children receive sensitive and appropriate adult intervention in their learning. However, this must be balanced against opportunities to work alone and in groups to consolidate, practise and apply their knowledge in a free play situation, for example, outdoors or in the role-play area.

Finally, remember that those children who are younger or who have special educational needs may not necessarily achieve all the goals by the end of the reception year. However, they should be able to participate fully in the wealth of mathematical experiences offered in the early years. All children irrespective of race, disability, gender and ethnic origin must be enabled to participate fully in the educational programme for Mathematical Development. In turn, this will enhance their development in each of the other areas of learning.

Links with other areas of learning

The Foundation Stage has six areas of learning which help you to plan the environment, activities and experiences. However, young children do not learn in subject compartments and the distinction between the areas is blurred at the edges.

One apparently simple experience in mathematics, for example, may cross skills and concepts in a number of areas. Consider, for example, children building with a variety of blocks or bricks on the floor, who may be:

❏ counting, comparing the size, weight and quantity or making patterns with the colours of the bricks (Mathematical Development);

❏ taking turns, concentrating, sharing and co-operating with others (Personal, Social and Emotional Development);

❏ questioning why things happen (Knowledge and Understanding of the World);

❏ speaking and listening to an adult or each other (Communication, Language and Literacy);

❏ building and constructing for a purpose (Knowledge and Understanding of the World);

❏ exploring shape in three-dimensional form (Creative Development);

❏ refining their manipulative skills (Physical Development).

A closer look at links between Mathematical Development and each of the other five areas illustrates the point that each area is interwoven. However, it is important in planning to decide to focus on the learning objective(s) of a planned activity rather than try to cover everything at once. You can link these objectives with assessment and future planning.

Personal, Social and Emotional Development

The goals for this learning area are not always obviously linked with Mathematical Development. However, a look beneath the surface shows a number of ways in which the two areas are intermeshed. The Early Learning Goals for Personal, Social and Emotional Development, for example, include helping children become motivated to learn. Mathematical experiences presented in attractive and enjoyable ways, such as through sand and water play, can certainly do this.

Experiences with puzzles such as number jigsaws or matching games will offer opportunities for children to 'maintain attention, concentrate and sit quietly when appropriate'. Setting up the role-play area with mathematical resources will encourage children to play co-operatively in small groups. The child who is the shopkeeper will develop a relationship with the customer. A maths table or a maths corner will allow children to 'select and use activities and resources independently'. Many mathematical games will help children to 'take turns and share fairly'.

Communication, Language and Literacy

In spite of the traditional divide between maths and English, the two areas are closely linked. Mathematics contains a wealth of vocabulary and extends children's ability to communicate in a variety of ways. Practical activities in mathematics must be underpinned by oral development and this will inevitably lead to gains in Communication, Language and Literacy. Communication, Language and Literacy can be divided into three broad areas - speaking and listening, reading and writing. Mathematics makes a contribution to all three areas. In speaking and listening, the use of mathematical language extends children's vocabulary. Mathematics introduces them to a range of words that will help them communicate effectively. This will help children:

❏ 'extend their vocabulary, exploring the meanings and sounds of new words'.

A number of the mathematical goals include words such as 'language', 'words', 'talk' and 'vocabulary', emphasising the importance of language in mathematics:

❏ 'use everyday words to describe position';

❏ 'use language such as 'greater', 'smaller', 'heavier' or 'lighter' to compare quantities;

❏ 'use language such as 'circle' or

'bigger' to describe the shape and size of solids and flat shapes';

❏ 'begin to use the vocabulary involved in addition and subtraction';

❏ 'talk about, recognise and recreate simple patterns'.

All these are closely related to a number of the Communication, Language and Literacy goals, such as 'explore and experiment with words'. Children will use mathematical vocabulary to do this. In mathematical problem-solving children will be applying the Communication, Language and Literacy goal to 'use talk to organise, sequence and clarify thinking, ideas, feelings and events'.

Children may be encouraged to 'speak clearly and audibly' as they name shapes and discuss new concepts such as 'heavy' and 'light'. They will 'listen with enjoyment and respond' to number rhymes, songs and stories. Number rhymes will also encourage children to understand how words rhyme together which is an essential part of spelling and reading. *Round and Round the Garden* by Sarah Williams is ideal for the nursery age group. Even old favourites such as 'Baa baa black sheep' help children learn linguistic as well as mathematical concepts, such as one-to-one correspondence as in 'One for the master, one for the dame and one for the little boy . . .'

Children are more likely to read and recall stories which are slightly different and contain a 'mathematical' or sequential element. When looking at books or listening to stories, draw children's attention to mathematical elements, for example, in the pictures. Many popular picture and story books relate to mathematical concepts, for example Eric Carle's *The Bad-Tempered Ladybird* and *The Very Hungry Caterpillar*. More traditional tales such as

'Goldilocks and the Three Bears' also involve concepts such as the comparison of size. A range of books relating to shape, size and colour will also encourage children's early reading skills. Those suitable for younger children include *I Can Count* (Ladybird) or Chuck Murphy's *A Rainbow Book of Numbers*.

Learning to discriminate between shapes and to sort and classify objects into groups will help children's visual discrimination in shapes of letters and words. The mathematical goal relating to patterns is also linked with Communication, Language and Literacy. Sequencing and pattern making in mathematics will help children to recognise and recreate patterns in spelling and reading. It will help them recognise and remember

sequences of events in stories and recurring patterns in words.

In Communication, Language and Literacy children are expected to:

❏ 'know that print carries meaning';

❏ 'attempt writing for a variety of purposes'.

Both goals overlap with aspects of Mathematical Development. As they begin to recognise numerals children will be learning that they are symbols for words; they carry meaning in the same way as the written word. The children will be writing for various purposes and audiences as they write letters and numbers on price lists, labels for the shop, addresses, telephone numbers and so on.

Other aspects of the Early Learning Goals such as 'use a pencil and hold it effectively' will occur later when children begin to form numbers.

Knowledge and Understanding of the World

The Early Learning Goals for Knowledge and Understanding of the World help children to understand the world in which they live and their place in it. Mathematics is actually incorporated into this area of learning in the Scottish Curriculum Framework (see page 5) and is probably more closely linked with this area than any other. Almost all the elements in this area of learning have some links with mathematics. One of the strongest links is with the goal which states that children will be able to:

❏ 'look closely at similarities, differences, patterns and change'.

In mathematics children are encouraged to sort everyday objects by certain properties, for example size, shape or colour. In order to do this they need to look closely at the objects and notice what is the same and what is different about them. Natural materials can be used for this purpose - sorting out leaves, conkers, classifying insects or animals. You can ask children to count the legs and spots on a ladybird, or the wings on a bird, the petals on a flower. Children can use magnifying glasses to examine patterns in rocks and leaves and shells or a butterfly's wing. Encourage them to recognise patterns in the world around them such as the stripes on a zebra crossing or patterns in bricks.

When they 'identify features in the place they live and the natural world' children will also discover all sorts of shapes, patterns and numbers. A project on 'Homes', for example,

could introduce different shaped windows, different patterns in wallpaper, different numbers of bedrooms. A walk to the local shops would prompt a wealth of mathematical experiences, questions and investigations.

Another goal in this area is to:

❏ 'find out about past and present events in their own lives, and in those of their families and other people they know.'

This will help children to understand the concept of time and to sequence events in a logical order. Children will develop important mathematical concepts, including problem-solving, as they:

❏ 'build and construct with a wide range of objects' and

❏ 'select the tools and techniques they need to shape, assemble and join the materials they are using'.

In Knowledge and Understanding of the World children are expected to be able to ask questions about why things happen and how things work. This is an essential part of mathematical development and problem-solving. How does a bicycle wheel turn? How do things balance? Why does the water tray overflow? Why do some things float and others sink?

This area also includes the use of information and communication technology. Programmable toys such as Roamer are often operated by numbers. There is a wide range of software available for children to use as a learning tool in mathematics. Popular topics for programs include number and shape recognition, counting and pattern making.

Creative Development

Although there are only five goals in this area of learning, some are intermeshed with the goals for Mathematical Development. In particular the goal which suggests that children will be able to:

❑ 'Explore colour, shape, form and space in two and three dimensions'.

Here, children will be learning to experiment with colours and shapes, gradually differentiating and sorting them into sets. In modelling, for example, they will begin to recognise the difference between two- and three-dimensional shapes. They will learn to observe patterns in art and make their own patterns in collage or when printing, painting and drawing.

Sand and water play is invaluable in exploring mathematical concepts relating to comparison of quantities. Experimenting with pasta, rice, jelly or cornflower also allows children to use their senses creatively. In music, too, children can be encouraged to use mathematical patterns as they clap rhythms or count beats with their instruments. Singing number rhymes will offer an opportunity for children to enjoy singing songs together.

In imaginative and role play many mathematical experiences will occur spontaneously. Children will sort and share, count and use mathematical language in role-play contexts such as the cafe, hospital or post office. They will stretch their imaginations as they practise and consolidate their mathematical knowledge and skills.

Physical Development

Aspects of Physical Development can be linked with Mathematical Development. When using 'a range of small and large equipment', children may apply their mathematical knowledge and understanding. They will recognise a ball as a sphere or a hoop as a circle. They may recognise the shape of a bicycle wheel. They will play with large and small balls and relate their concept of size to this equipment. They will be able to count the number of steps on the slide, the number of skips or the number of throws. Various physical games involve counting or scoring, for example skittles and mini-rounders.

There are also a number of mathematical elements in the Early Learning Goal which expects children to be able to:

❑ 'travel around, under, over and through balancing and climbing equipment'.

This is linked to the mathematical goal of using positional language. On an obstacle course, for example, children will learn to use and understand words such as 'under' and 'over'. The concept of balance will be reinforced as children explore their bodies' capabilities of balancing and transference of weight. In movement, too, children will use their awareness of patterns such as hop, skip, jump, hop, skip, jump and so on.

Activities to promote number skills

Stories, songs and rhymes

Board games and puzzles

Large and small construction play

Cooking

Model making

Exploring patterns

Mathematical Development

The importance of play

In spite of the tradition of mathematics being a formal subject in the school curriculum it is important to recognise that play and mathematics are not mutually exclusive. On the contrary, children will learn mathematics through their play and they will learn to play through their mathematical experiences.

Well-planned play is essential for children to deepen their understanding of mathematics in the Foundation Stage. This includes play both indoors and outdoors. Early years workers need to consider some fundamental questions.

❑ What is play?

❑ Why is it important for young children to learn through play?

❑ What contribution can play activities make to children's mathematical development?

Play will provide unique opportunities for children to develop mathematical knowledge, skills, attitudes and understanding.

Through play children will come to realise that mathematics is useful and enjoyable. They will be motivated to learn. They will begin to understand that it is a powerful tool for communication. They will learn that mathematics is useful in everyday situations such as shopping. Mathematical play also offers children opportunities to apply their

knowledge in problem-solving situations. It provides a safe environment for children to:

❑ practise and consolidate concepts and skills;

❑ talk to, communicate and collaborate with others;

❑ clarify ideas;

❑ develop confidence;

❑ think creatively and imaginatively.

All work and no play

The distinction between play and work is best explained by thinking of play as something where children initiate the task; work is when they do a task required by an adult. Imagine these scenarios:

Scene 1

An adult chooses four children to come and sit at a table. The adult brings a basket of cubes and a set of numeral cards. She gives each child a card with a number on and takes one for herself. She builds a tower to correspond with the number on her card. She instructs the children to do the same on their cards.

Scene 2

The children fetch a box of wooden bricks and tip them on the floor. The children build towers with the bricks and begin to count the number of bricks in their towers spontaneously. They talk to each other saying, 'I've got five! How many have you got?'

Scene 3

As in scene 2, but an adult begins to join in the play. She is careful not to dominate but asks the children questions such as 'Which tower do you think has the most bricks?', 'Why do you think that?', 'How many would you have if you put two more on?', 'Let's try and see.' The adult withdraws. The children carry on.

Scene 4

All 30 children in the group sit at tables. They each have a worksheet with numbers on and pictures of brick towers. With a pencil they all are instructed to join up the number to the tower and then colour in the towers.

It is important to consider the style and quality of teaching and learning taking place in each scene. Each raises issues relating to mathematics and play. The first scene is essentially a teacher directed activity. It is not play but nevertheless may be useful in assessing what the children know or teaching them to recognise numbers and to count. They could then move on to explore the ideas in their play.

In scene 2, the children play independently and spontaneously. It is appropriate to leave them alone and observe at this stage. Each of these scenes could follow the previous one. In scene 3 an observing adult has judged it appropriate to join in and extend children's language and thinking, but is careful not to dominate. The final scenario is very formal, uninspiring and not appropriate for the Foundation Stage. A large group of children learn at vastly differing rates and will be at different ages and stages. They will learn little from this exercise although they will have the sheet to take home! It may look as if they have done some 'work' - but has it met their individual learning needs?

Play provides an environment where the child feels free from pressure and ensures activity rests on a practical rather than a written focus. A key point raised in these scenes is that the adults should be continually observing children as they play and sensitively intervening to gently reinforce and extend the children's understanding. The early years worker needs the skill of sharing in a child's play without dominating. However, it is equally important not to leave a child struggling. In other words, the adult needs to recognise when a child needs help and when she needs to be left alone. The adult role in a play situation is to:

❑ observe,

❑ support, and

❑ extend.

It is also important for the adult to recognise where the mathematics is within the play activities. Settings should provide a variety of mathematical experiences, some of which will be adult led, others will be a result of children's free choice. The important point is that the activities match the children's level of understanding.

Role play

Role play is a common feature in pre-school settings and given high priority in the Ofsted nursery inspection framework. However, it is primarily associated with the areas of Communication, Language and Literacy or Creative Development. Nevertheless, a well-planned, appropriately resourced role-play area can offer a wealth of mathematical experiences in pre-school and in Reception classes.

If, for example, the role-play area is organised as a shop, children might sort out the various packets and tins

into shelves or shopping baskets. This would involve sorting, matching and comparing as well as recognising the shapes and sizes of the various containers. They would handle solid shapes such as boxes, tubes and tins. Price lists would promote number recognition. The shopkeepers could explore balance and compare measures using weighing scales. If provided with writing materials they can begin to record numbers by writing their own bills or receipts for customers. They will need to count the number of items required by the customer. The customer would use mathematical language to ask for a 'small bottle of tomato sauce' or 'two kilos of sugar'. Customers can write shopping lists and use old cheque books to write cheques. Resources such as telephones, tills and calculators will also help children use and recognise numbers in a practical situation. Through these types of experience children make sense of their own real-life experiences and build up a range of mathematical concepts.

Water play

This is particularly important in mathematics. It offers children the chance to explore and experiment with capacity. It stimulates the use of mathematical vocabulary and, most importantly, the children really enjoy

it. A large water tray is ideal but a washing-up bowl shared between a small group of children is better than nothing at all. Resources for good quality water play include items of varying shapes, sizes and colours. You could use margarine tubs, plastic bottles and cups, plastic spoons, funnels, sieves, yoghurt pots and so on.

Adult-led activities might include emptying and filling a number of plastic bottles of varying sizes and encouraging the children to order them. Coloured water is useful in this context. Whilst playing independently children will begin to compare the amounts of water the various containers hold. A supply of various shapes and sizes will encourage them to use mathematical language such as 'more' and 'most', 'empty' and 'full'. They may discover how many small cups of water they need to fill a jug, or how many spoons to fill a cup.

Independent play

Children should have access to a variety of play materials. Almost all of these will have some value in mathematical learning through play. Pattern making will occur through construction play, where children sequence coloured bricks, or through bead threading. Children will compare heights and lengths as they build with bricks or blocks. They will look at curves and straights as they construct a railway track or they may count the carriages. Farm or zoo animals will be sorted or partitioned into groups. Children will have to think about sizes as they dress the dolls. Various shapes will be encountered as they play with houses and garages.

It is important to observe children and note significant uses of mathematical language, numbers and so on during independent play. Often children will apply what they know in this situation but not have the same opportunity to show it in an adult-led activity. For example, a child may be observed putting socks on a family of dolls and count the legs - 'Two and another two and another two and another two, that makes eight altogether'. Then he thinks for a moment and says 'Oh, look! There are eight legs, the same as a spider. I need eight socks.' This tells you he knows that a number is the amount in the set, he is using simple addition, he is beginning to count in twos and recognise pattern in number.

Table top and floor games

Children enjoy counting games such as those involving dice. Younger children will probably need the support of an adult in games with turn taking and simple rules. You should aim to provide a wide range of table top and floor games. Younger children could play games with a large foam dice with spots. Older children can use large dice with numerals and then smaller dice. Eventually, they can use two dice and add the numbers together. Every time the child moves the counter she is practising counting.

Children can learn and practise as they play a variety of games or puzzles which involve matching or making pairs. These might range from giant floor dominoes with coloured dots for younger children to ordinary dominoes for older ones. Some dominoes have only spots, others have numbers and spots or pictures. This helps match the play to the children's level of understanding. Other popular choices are bingo or a class lottery.

Puzzles which involve one-to-one correspondence, such as matching together a cup and saucer, knife and fork, bucket and spade, and so on, are also popular and enjoyable. Those based on matching opposites will introduce mathematical concepts relating to size and comparison.

Games involving physical activity often help children to use and remember numbers. There are scoring games such as skittles, mini-golf and children's darts or try throwing bean bags into a bucket and counting how many out of five land in the bucket, how many land on the floor. Adapt traditional games such as hopscotch, five stones, follow my leader, hunt the thimble or Simon says to emphasise elements of mathematical language and number concepts.

Finally, the Early Learning Goals document states that the practitioner's role in play is crucial in:

Basic resource list for mathematical development

Number lines/friezes

Collection of objects for sorting and classifying

Solid and flat shapes

Calculators

Unifix and Multilink cubes

Threading beads

Peg boards

Timers

Mirrors

Containers of various shapes and sizes

Tape measures/rulers

Dominoes

Games/puzzles/books

Balances and scales

Numbers (plastic or wooden)

Coins

❑ planning and resourcing a challenging environment;

❑ supporting children's learning through planned play activity;

❑ extending and supporting children's spontaneous play;

❑ extending and developing children's language and communication in their play.

With a little imagination and a lot of play, maths can be fun!

Let's make patterns!

Children are interested in patterns from an early age - whether it be when they tip all their yoghurt onto the high-chair and swirl their finger in it or when they repeatedly insist on playing 'pat-a-cake'! Patterns are all around us but often pass unnoticed. However, not all patterns are mathematical. In the Foundation Stage children need planned opportunities to explore and discover those that are.

The Early Learning Goal suggests that by the end of the reception year children should achieve three elements relating to mathematical patterns. They should be able to:

❑ talk about pattern;

❑ recognise a pattern;

❑ recreate simple patterns.

Some aspects of these three elements may occur simultaneously. However, most children will need to talk about and understand what a pattern is before progressing to the recognition stage, and then to recreate a given pattern. Once they have achieved these three elements children will consolidate their knowledge by independently and deliberately creating their own patterns. Usually,

activities to provide experience in this area need to be planned. However, this does not mean they always need to be adult directed or 'taught'. Children need the opportunity to explore and create patterns for themselves with the adult sensitively intervening when necessary.

A mathematical pattern may involve:

❑ a sequence which is repeated and which, once the pattern is recognised, can be predicted and replicated; a very simple mathematical pattern which can be made with coloured bricks arranged alternately, for example red, yellow, red, yellow;

❑ a matching pattern where the shape is reflected; these can be made by folding 'blob' paintings or by folding paper and cutting;

❑ a growing pattern where a number or shape is increased or decreased by the same amount each time, such as when building towers with barrels of increasing size or circles inside each other; also in number rhymes going down or up one at a time.

Talking about patterns

Make the most of opportunities to talk about patterns. This can be done in a number of ways. However, as with most areas of learning, it is more effective to begin with real objects, things which have meaning for the children. Small group discussion activities based around observing and talking about the nature of the patterns are a good introduction. Some of the following natural and made resources can prompt discussion:

Early Learning Goal

❑ Talk about, recognise and recreate simple patterns.

Wrapping paper; wallpaper; curtain material; pillowcases; patchwork; hats and scarves; tea towels; tablecloths; dish cloths; jumpers; pyjamas; dresses; plates, cups and saucers; drinking straws; shells; leaves; stones; bricks.

Provide a magnifying glass for the children to examine the similarities and differences between the patterns more closely. Ask the children questions. 'Which pattern do you like the best?' 'What do you like about it?' 'What do you notice about the flowers?' 'What do you notice about this scarf?' 'Can you see a pattern on anyone's clothes?' 'Tell me something about the pattern on this tea towel.' 'Can you see another one with the same pattern?' 'Can you find the other piece of wallpaper to match this one?' You could arrange a day when the children come in wearing something with a pattern on or have a 'pattern table' where they can display things brought in from home.

Encourage children to notice patterns in their environment, indoors and outdoors. Indoors, for example, there may be patterns on the windows, doors, carpets, furniture, bean bags or wall tiles. You could take the children outdoors on pattern hunt. Talk to them and encourage them to notice the different patterns in garden walls, fencing, house bricks and paving slabs, on flowers, leaves and so on. What about the pattern in a traffic light sequence or on a zebra crossing.

It is important continually to point out the nature of the pattern. Begin with a simple repeated sequence and move on to more complex patterns as children learn to talk about the patterns themselves. You could display books and posters with pictures of animals or insects with patterned features - butterflies, ladybirds, snakes, tigers and zebras. Introduce children to artistic patterns from other cultures. Look at and talk about paintings. Read the story of Elmer the Elephant.

You can also encourage children to notice and talk about patterns as they play independently, for example, with construction equipment. As they draw, paint, print or create collage they may begin to create patterns. Number stamps and an ink pad in the post office role-play area will encourage children to create patterns with numerals - 1, 2, 3; 1, 2, 3.

Recreating patterns

Allow the children to play with beads and lace, making snakes and necklaces. Talk with them about the colours they have chosen. Some children may spontaneously begin to thread red, blue, red, blue. Be explicit in pointing out the patterns they are making. Say things such as 'Oh, look! Ryan's made a pattern! Red, blue, red, blue. What colour do you think he will need next? Let's see if we can work it out - red, blue, red, blue. Will it be red or blue?' Point to the pattern and ask the children to tell you the sequence.

Move the children on to more complex arrangements as they become more skilled and experienced, for example two red, one blue or a greater combination of colours such as red, yellow, green, red, yellow, green. The same could be done with reels, buttons, pegboards or coloured wooden bricks.

Let the children take turns to be the leader. One child builds a tower and the others try to build one with the same pattern. Provide some pre-arranged patterns on a card or a pegboard for the children to copy and continue. 'See if you can thread your necklace the same as this one.' Talk about what they need to do. 'Which one are you going to put on first? What next?'

Assessment

It is important to observe and check the children understand that patterns are about relationships and involve order and repetition.

❑ Can the child recognise a pattern?

❑ Can the child talk about a pattern?

❑ Can the child copy a pattern?

❑ Can the child predict what comes next in a given pattern?

❑ Can the child create his own patterns?

Older children may be able to make patterns, for example, with Unifix cubes and then record the pattern onto squared paper. Challenge them by asking: 'How many different patterns can you make with these cubes?' You could then lead on to other sequences of repeating patterns with properties other than number or colour. For example, alternate shapes: blue triangle, yellow circle ...

Children can paint, draw or use collage work to recreate or make their own patterns. Commercial resources such as Linking Elephants are more abstract but an excellent resource for both adult-led activities and free play.

All these experiences will help children to recognise and use patterns in numbers in other areas of learning, for example two big steps, one little step, two big steps; hop, skip, hop, skip. Encourage them to talk about, recognise, copy and create sound patterns in music - beating on a drum or tambourine: loud, loud, quiet; loud, loud, quiet. Clapping - one, two and three, four; one, two and three, four. Walking - quick, quick, slow.

Measuring up

The Early Learning Goals suggest that children will be expected to use mathematical language to compare two numbers or quantities. This introduces children to the early stages of measurement. Using mathematical language in this way will enable children to begin to use the mathematical vocabulary associated with measuring height, weight, time, speed, distance, capacity, area and numbers of objects which can be counted. The important aspect at the Foundation Stage is the language of comparison, not the specific units of measurement which can be used at a later stage.

Comparing two numbers focuses on numbers in a set and relates closely to counting skills. However, estimating may also be involved. For example, by the end of the reception year a child should be able to guess which box contains the most apples without counting. She may also be able to predict which empty container would hold the most.

Children should be introduced to groups of mathematical words including:

❑ long, longer, longest

❑ short, shorter shortest

❑ tall, taller, tallest

❑ heavy, heavier heaviest

❑ light, lighter, lightest

❑ more than, less than

❑ most, fewest

❑ empty, full

❑ wide, narrow

❑ fast, faster,

❑ slow, slower

Some activities involving the language of comparison will occur as children

---

Early Learning Goals

These activities will help you work towards the following goals:

❑ Use language such as 'more' or 'less' to compare two numbers.

❑ Use language such as 'circle' or 'bigger' to describe the shape and size of solid and flat shapes.

❑ Use language such as 'greater', 'smaller', 'heavier' or 'lighter' to compare quantities.

❑ Use developing mathematical ideas and methods to solve practical problems.

---

play independently, for example you could encourage children to compare the height of brick towers by asking 'Who has made the tallest tower?' When playing with the zoo animals, you could ask 'Which animal is the tallest?' 'Is the giraffe taller than the elephant?' 'Which do you think is heavier?' Other chances may arise from regular planned activities such as measuring or weighing ingredients whilst baking cakes. How does 50 grammes of sugar compare in size to 50 grammes of butter? Children will learn about comparing measures as they play with tape measures, scales, clocks, sand timers, and so on. They will learn about capacity as they play with various size containers in the water tray.

Popular activities such as growing tomato plants or sunflowers are also ideal for encouraging children to measure and record measurement. Younger children may, for example, measure the height by counting the number of bricks up the wall the flower has grown. Older children might use coloured strips of paper or centimetre cubes. In measuring children need to grasp the idea of counting regularly increasing intervals. One spoonful, two spoonfuls, three spoonfuls is an increasing measure of quantity. One hand span, two hand spans, three hand spans is an increasing measure of distance.

It is important to provide a balance between child-initiated activities where children can consolidate and experiment and concepts 'taught' through adult-directed activities. The adult plays an important role in promoting mathematical language and thinking because they can introduce new concepts and associated vocabulary. Effective questioning allows children to develop their understanding of comparisons of quantity and measures in a meaningful context.

Heavy and light

A useful starting point is to introduce the words and concept of 'heavy' and 'light' to children. Sit a small group around a table or on the carpet in a circle. Take a group of objects, some heavy and some light, such as a stone, a bunch of keys, piece of paper, book, feather.

Let each child pick up an object. Talk about whether the children think the object is heavy or light. Ask questions and give prompts such as:

❑ 'Do you think that is heavy?' 'Yes, it is heavy isn't it? You have to be strong to carry that, don't you?'

❑ 'Now, what about this feather. Is it heavy?' 'No, it's light.'

❑ 'Can you find something else on the table which is light?'

Children can then pick up one heavy and one light object in each hand and you could ask them to say which is heavy and which is light.

Play a game

Put an assortment of light and heavy objects in a box or bag. Ask the children in turn to feel in the bag and choose an object. Before they take it out of the bag, encourage each child to say whether they think their object is heavy or light.

This can be done firstly with a few objects which are easily compared. Then reduce the discrepancy between the objects and increase the number to select from. Once you think the children have grasped the idea and they are using the appropriate language, see if they can sort a given group of objects into heavy and light - all the heavy books in one box, all the light ones in another, for example. Older children could record their observations by drawing or sticking pictures into heavy and light sets.

For those who learn more quickly, ask challenging questions such as:

❑ 'Which do you think is heavier?'

❑ 'Which is lighter?'

❑ 'Which is lightest?'

Once children understand the concept of heavy and light, move them on by encouraging them to hold two objects, one in each hand, so that they use their hands as a balance and feel which is heavier/lighter. You can then introduce them to balancing scales and weighing familiar objects such as conkers, marbles, Sticklebricks or toy cars. Ask questions such as 'Do we need to make it heavier to make it balance or lighter?' 'Do we need to

> **Assessment**
>
> It is important to check that the child can use the language of comparison in everyday situations.
>
> ❑ Does the child use words such as 'heavier' or 'taller'?
>
> ❑ Can the child sort by comparison of quantity?
>
> ❑ Can the child say which container holds the most water?
>
> ❑ Can the child identify the tallest tower?
>
> ❑ Can the child identify the longest snake?

put more conkers in or take some out to make it balance?'

Set up an interactive display of different types of weighing scales which might include simple balances, kitchen scales, bathroom scales, a spring balance and digital display baking scales. Let the children play and consolidate their understanding by weighing the dolls, teddy bears, fruit in the fruit shop, parcels in the post office, and so on. Let them experiment by pouring sand or sugar through a plastic funnel into the bucket scales and seeing what happens to the buckets.

In a practical way the concept of comparison could be extended to sort or order groups of three objects into heavy, heavier, heaviest or light, lighter, lightest. Children could move on to order small numbers of objects from the lightest to the heaviest. Check understanding in the abstract by asking if they think an elephant is heavy or light. It is this type of adult questioning which encourages children to think mathematically and to become familiar with the use of mathematical terms.

Getting into shape

From an early age children play with shape sorters, pushing the shapes through the appropriate hole. They build towers with wooden bricks or cubes. This is extended through the popular 'Shape' topic in many early years settings. However, the potential mathematical learning which can be developed is often not fully realised. It can be restricted to sorting and naming flat shapes when it is much broader than this.

'Shape' is an excellent cross-curricular topic. Many aspects can be incorporated and consolidated through other subjects or areas of learning. In Reception classes, for example, a 'Shape' topic may be planned in PE. In the nursery, children may be encouraged to look for shapes in the environment as a part of Knowledge and Understanding of the World. Yet surprisingly few children are given the opportunity to look for similarities and differences between shapes using natural and made materials, such as bricks or block paving slabs. In Creative Development, children can explore how shapes can be changed and reflected by cutting, folding, rotating or turning. They can use shapes to cover an area and learn that some shapes fit together without spaces in collage work. Shapes can be used for printing and pattern-making purposes - designing wallpaper, bubble painting or tie and dye. In Communication, Language and Literacy children can look at books about shape or extend their vocabulary as they talk about shapes. Careful planning will make achieving this goal interesting and fun.

Using language

The Early Learning Goal relating specifically to shape is:

❑ 'use language such as 'circle' or 'bigger' to describe the shape and size of solid and flat shapes'.

This links closely with skills defined in the national numeracy strategy which states that children should be taught to:

❑ 'use language to describe the shape and size of solid and flat shapes, begin to name them and use them to make models, pictures and patterns.'

This appears straightforward but the underpinning knowledge and understanding to achieve this goal is more complex. In order to learn to recognise shapes, distinguish one shape from another and use shape names such as 'circle', children need to know the names of the other common flat and solid shapes:

❑ triangle

❑ circle

❑ square

Early Learning Goals

These activities will help you work towards the following goal:

❑ Use language such as 'circle' or 'bigger' to describe the shape and size of solid and flat shapes.

❑ rectangle

❑ cube

❑ cuboid

❑ sphere

❑ cylinder

They will also need to learn the language which will help them recognise and describe the properties of one shape as compared to another. It is not only a matter of comparing size. Children need experiences which will help them learn to classify or sort shapes for a variety of criteria. This will involve words such as:

❑ edge

❑ side

❑ corner

❑ face

❑ straight

❑ round

Once the particular shape is named you know that the child has drawn together all the properties of that shape and is able to use that one shape name to identify that shape and all its properties as distinct from any other shape.

Starting points

You can introduce children to the basic shapes by looking at them and naming them. The circle is a good starting point for investigating similarities and differences in shapes as it is more easily distinguishable from the rest. A good introduction is to look for shapes in the environment - two-dimensional such as windows, doors, table mats; three-dimensional everyday objects such as sweet tubes, tins, balls, bricks. Begin to encourage the children to talk about the properties of a particular shape. 'Look at this window; it's a square shape.' 'How many corners can you see?' 'How many sides?' 'Are they the same?' 'Are the edges straight or round?' 'Now look at this one (repeat questions).' 'Is it a circle?' 'Why not?' 'So what shape do you think it is?' 'Let's see if we can find any more square windows.'

In the classroom shape puzzles and games such as shape dominoes or shape lotto encourage and consolidate important skills such as matching shapes on a one-to-one basis. The most important question in the early stages is, 'Can you find another one like this?'

Construction play

Construction play offers a wealth of mathematical experiences which will encourage children to use mathematical language relating to shape. Children need to experiment with various types of 3-d shapes including:

❏ blocks

❏ bricks

❏ polydrons

❏ modelling from recycled materials

The vocabulary needs to be introduced in meaningful contexts. Adults should build alongside the children, talking all the time about what they are doing. As children build houses, castles, boats and planes they will be learning about the size and properties of the shapes and matching like with like. Adults may help by asking questions such as, 'Do you need some more big bricks?' or 'Would a small brick fit there?' 'What shape do you need for the wheel?' 'Which shape will make a good tower?'

Junk modelling

In making models from recycled materials such as cereal boxes and cardboard rolls children explore and discover the properties of the shapes. They notice which shapes are the same and different, which ones fit together, how many corners the box has, and so on. Adults can help children make decisions by asking relevant questions such as 'Do you think this will make a good wheel?' and challenge them to think: 'Why not?' or 'What shape do you need for the door?' 'Is that the same shape as a real door?'

Ideas for display

Collect objects of particular shapes and create a shape table. This could be changed or added to from week to week. Familiar objects are essential. On a circle week, for example, you might have a tambourine, bracelets, buttons, a hoop, a round shape cutter and small wheels. The next week you could add cylinders, including various sizes and lengths of tins and tubes. This will help children grasp the idea that a sweet tube, a cotton reel and a tin of beans are all cylindrical.

On the wall you could have four opening cardboard windows. Each day ask the children 'Which window shall we look inside today?' Look behind the square window and see squares of various sizes and colours.

Shape week

Although children will learn about different shapes in various contexts, it is useful to focus on particular shapes to establish a firmer understanding. Each week, for example, a variety of activities could be planned around a specific shape. If it were circle week, children could come in one day wearing clothes with circles on. They could make pizzas and eat round biscuits. They could look for circles in the nursery or classroom and add them to the circle table - which could also be a circle. Organise craftwork around printing or collage with circles. Outdoors you could play circle or ring games or focus on hoops. Take groups out to look for circles in the environment such as road signs. It is important for children to understand that circles can be of different sizes, so make a collection of big and small circles. Play games that involve picking the circle from a group of shapes, beginning with contrasting shapes such as squares and progressing to similar shapes such as ovals. Make up games such as 'Find the odd one out' or 'I spy with my little eye something that has no corners'. Provide circular paper at the painting easel and see if they notice. Similar activities could be organised for the other shapes.

Shape hunt

This can be organised in a number of ways. At first, you could just play 'Find the shape'. Start with one specific shape. Show the children the ones you are going to hide and let them find them. Then make it more difficult by hiding them without the children seeing them first. Then hide two different shapes, for example squares and circles. Ask the children to tell you which shape or shapes they have found. You could give clues such as 'I have hidden a shape with four corners and four straight edges'. Then let the children hide the shapes for each other to find.

Another popular variation is the feely box or bag. Children put a hand in and have to guess the size and shape they are picking out. If the child picks out a triangle, discuss the properties. 'Does it have three or four sides?' 'If it has three it must be a ... ?' 'Is it a big triangle or a small triangle?'

Capitalise on spontaneous opportunities during the daily routine to talk about shape and size with the children. Use the proper shape names from the beginning. If they can remember the names of dinosaurs and all of Thomas the Tank Engine's friends, they can learn the names of the shapes!

Catering for different abilities

It is important to adjust the activities and the amount of adult support in order to cater for children who learn more quickly or more slowly. If you say to an older child 'Tell me about what you have made', she should be able to explain clearly, 'I've made a garage. The windows are square.' If you ask, 'What are you going to do next?' she might say 'I'm going to make the roof with this because I need four corners and straight edges for the roof'.

You could provide younger children with a selection of shapes for them to choose from to make random 2-d and

3-d shape patterns or collages. They will need more adult modelling of the vocabulary involved. 'What shape is this one?' 'Has it got any corners?' 'Is it round?' 'Is it a circle?' 'Can you find another circle?'

Provide playdough and a range of shape cutters. With younger children talk about the various shapes that they make and the properties of those shapes. Older children could be expected to begin to name the shapes they are making or could explore drawing round shape templates on the drawing table. Ask them, 'Is it a triangle?' 'How do you know it's not a triangle?' The main purpose is to encourage children to use the language involved in describing the properties of shapes. In this way, they will eventually know the shape names.

Working with a cube

Introducing faces

With younger children the objective should be to introduce the idea of a shape with faces. Put a selection of cubes into a box or bag. These might include several bricks the same size, several bricks of different sizes and some sugar cubes. Explain to the children that you are going to look at some special shapes. Show them the brick and see if anyone knows the name. They may say 'square'. You could then build on this, saying, 'No, it's not a square. But, yes, you can see a square. Show me the square. This is a special shape because it has square faces. A shape with square faces is called a cube. Let's all say that together.' You could even draw eyes, nose and mouth to encourage the use of the word 'face' when talking about 3-d shapes.

Then move on to look at another brick the same size but perhaps a different colour. Ask again: 'Now look at this; it's the same shape. What sort of faces does this shape have?' 'Square, yes. So what shape do you think it is? Is it the same as the yellow one?'

Go on to count the faces. Explain clearly: 'Now we know two things about cubes - they have square faces and they have six faces altogether'. Show them another cube. 'Is this a cube?' Then give each child a ready-made cube and let them draw the faces on each face. Another popular activity for younger children would be to make dice or jack-in-the boxes. You could also make ice cubes to reinforce this activity.

Describing solid shapes

With older children your objective could be

to describe the size and shape of solid shapes. Remind them of the language by looking at a house brick. 'What can you tell me about this brick?' Put a selection of three-dimensional shapes in the centre of the table - objects such as cereal boxes, dice, tins, tubes can be used to practise sorting solid shapes. Ask the children to pick out a shape each. Say 'Who can tell me something about their shape?' Ask questions such as 'Who has a shape with six faces?' 'Who has a shape like a ball?' 'Who has a shape with corners?' 'Who has a shape with square faces?' 'How many corners has your shape got?'

See if they can find another shape the same as the one they chose. Ask them to find another shape in the room which is the same as theirs. Each child should have three shapes by this stage. Then ask them to put them on the table in size order from the smallest to the biggest. They could then use 3-d shapes to make patterns by threading onto string or to make models.

Exploring number

Understanding numbers is at the heart of mathematical development. From an early age children encounter number concepts informally as they share their sweets or give out their party bags. They begin to partition as they build with bricks. When children start school or nursery, there may be a temptation to present number work in worksheet format or as something to be learned by rote. Whilst these more formal methods have a part to play later on they are inappropriate in nursery and should be used sparingly, if at all, in Reception.

Several of the Early Learning Goals relate directly to number in one way or another, for example, 'count reliably up to ten everyday objects'. However, there is far more to number than counting. Reciting number names in the correct order is not enough on its own. When planning activities for promoting the Early Learning Goals,

number can be divided into six basic areas. Activities and experiences which help children:

❏ to understand the purpose of counting, in other words to find out how many there are in a set or group;

❏ to repeat numbers in the correct order;

❏ to count using one-to-one correspondence, in other words know that each object is only counted once;

❏ to understand that the last number in the set indicates the number, regardless of how the objects are arranged;

❏ to know what number comes before or after another number;

❏ to count reliably.

Many everyday activities and experiences discussed throughout this book contribute towards the learning of number. Resources and activities should be provided for spontaneous and planned learning both indoors and outdoors.

Spontaneous learning will occur in activities such as role play (see pages 36-39), construction play, use of interactive displays such as the body in an 'All about me' topic (see pages 58-59) as well as in counting and matching games, jigsaw puzzles, and through providing interesting objects for sorting and classifying (see pages 32-35). Opportunities will also occur in the daily routine, such as counting how

many children there are that day or how many children are allowed in the home corner. When you hear children say, 'Miss, there's five in the house and there's only four allowed!' you know they are beginning to apply their knowledge of number and have realised several things:

❏ the number is the last number in the set;

❏ what four means;

❏ the idea of one more;

❏ the idea of too many;

❏ what five means;

❏ one more than four is five.

Planned activities involving numeral cards such as 'Ten green bottles' (see pages 54-55) will help children understand that a number said is the number in the set. The number washing line (see page 41) and number friezes will help children realise what number comes next. Number rhymes and stories are an invaluable way to practise:

❏ saying the number names in order;

❏ counting one-to-one;

❏ finding one more or one less than a number from one to ten;

❏ using language involved in adding or subtracting.

Early Learning Goals

These activities will help you work towards the following goals:

❏ Say and use number names in order in familiar contexts.

❏ Count reliably up to ten everyday objects.

❏ Recognise numerals 1 to 9.

❏ In practical activities and discussion begin to use the vocabulary involved in adding and subtracting.

❏ Find one more or one less than a number from 1 to 10.

Number rhymes

Rhymes, games and songs allow children to rehearse saying number names in the right order as part of daily routine. You could display a list of popular number rhymes in the areas where you sing or plan a mini-topic around one of the rhymes. Number rhymes should be interactive. Some ideas are:

❑ Making finger puppets, for example of the five speckled frogs.

❑ Using Velcro-backed pictures and a display board, for example to take off one duck at a time from the pond in 'Five little ducks'.

❑ Involving the children, for example as a customer in 'Five currant buns'.

❑ Making up your own number rhymes and displays to fit in with your theme or adapting the words to traditional rhymes.

Younger children can be introduced to simple rhymes involving small numbers up to five and counting forwards. Older children's learning can be extended by counting backwards or by changing the words of those going to or from ten and counting in twos instead. Older children could hold up numerals instead of pictures.

Popular number rhymes

'Once I caught a fish alive'

'Five fat sausages'

'Five little speckled frogs'

'Alice the camel'

'Five little ducks'

'Five little men in a flying saucer'

'This old man, he played one'

'Ten in the bed'

'Five little monkeys jumping on the bed'

'Two little dicky birds'

Counting for a purpose

Adults need to provide role models and be explicit when they are counting for a purpose. They also need to provide planned opportunities such as cookery to help children count for a reason. One reason for counting is to check when an exact number is required, for example, 'There are four children in the sand tray'. This could be presented as a picture and numeral for the younger children. Secondly, children count to see how many there are - 'I've got three and he's got four'. At the early stage they come and tell you, 'I'm three!' (although they hold up four fingers!) or count one, two, three, four, seven, eight, ten. To assess a child's ability, ask them to fetch six plates or five cups and observe what they do.

Make a book of numbers

What you need:

Sugar paper (for book covers)

Large sheets of white or coloured paper

Scissors

Glue

Numeral templates (for example felt or gummed paper)

Variety of sets of clear pictures (cut from magazines, catalogues, or use photographs)

Compiling their own number book is a useful and enjoyable way for children to explore numbers in symbolic (numeral) and iconic (pictorial) form and keep a record of their own. It does not need to be made all at the same time but can be added to week by week.

Work though the numbers one by one. Check the children can recognise the numerals nought to nine. Divide the page into two. The numeral can then be glued at the top and the correct number of pictures glued underneath. With younger children you could use one page for the numeral and the opposite page for the pictorial representation. Explain clearly to the children what they are expected to do. Use a real book as an example or make one first to show them. Have a few trial runs at various numbers. Then let them begin with one and two. Ask the children to choose the correct number of pictures from those available. They may associate numbers with specific characteristics, for example two and eyes or just be more general - two apples, two dogs. Emergent writers may write their own numeral and/or caption on the page.

When all the pages are finished, tie or staple the pages together with a front and back cover. The final product will look something like a scrap book. It will be different for every child. They can keep the book and share it with friends in the book corner.

As a class or group the children could make mini-books for popular number rhymes or a big class book where different groups have contributed one or two rhymes.

A wide range of mathematical experiences will ensure most children learn to:

❑ understand number concepts;

❑ know number facts;

❑ solve number problems.

Assessment

❑ Does the child count accurately?

❑ Can the child bring a given number of an object?

❑ Does the child use numbers in play situations and daily routines?

❑ Does the child understand the number is the same when the objects being counted are rearranged into a different position?

Sorting and matching

The ability to sort and classify is an important aspect of mathematical development. Early number experiences are based on sets of objects - counting them, matching numerals to sets, matching sets to numerals, making patterns with different colours and/or shapes. Sorting is the first step towards logical thinking and has strong links with patterns, shape and number. It is a predecessor to the skill of sorting numbers, for example, into odd and even, or into those which divide by five. Classifying objects into sets also forms the basis of early addition, subtraction and comparison of size or number. As Pound (1999) points out, mathematics 'is fundamentally concerned with differences and similarities'. (Pound, pages 40-41)

puzzles

building bricks

Sorting can be divided into three key aspects, as children sort:

❑ by mathematical criteria such as shape, size, quantity, pattern, for example big bricks from little bricks;

❑ by common criteria, for example things that float, things that fly;

❑ as part of information or data handling, for example six children with blue eyes, three children like cornflakes.

The Desirable Learning Outcomes document (SCAA 1996) included an element suggesting that, by the age of

five, children should compare, sort, match and sequence everyday objects. Although not phrased in a specific Early Learning Goal these skills are implicit in most aspects of the area of Mathematical Development. For example, children could not achieve the goal relating to describing flat and solid shapes if they had not first learned to sort and classify those shapes by their properties.

Starting points

Children need to distinguish between same and different but then also to understand that things can be the same as each other as well as different from each other at the same time. Giving them experiences which encourage them to observe closely is important. Stand two children next to each other. Ask the other children

questions such as 'What can you see that is the same about Yasmin and Alice?' They may both have brown eyes or blue sweatshirts. 'Who else thinks they have something the same as

Early Learning Goals

These activities will help you work towards the following goals:

❑ Count reliably up to ten everyday objects.

❑ Use language such as 'greater', 'smaller', 'heavier' or 'lighter' to compare quantities.

❑ Use developing mathematical ideas and methods to solve practical problems.

Alice?' 'What is different about them?' 'Why do you think that they have different hair?' Play games such as 'Simon says' to develop children's awareness of 'the same' or 'Find the odd one out' for 'different'. It is important for children to say why they think certain items are the same or different.

Sorting the socks

You will need:

Selection of odd socks

Empty containers

Dolls or teddy bears

Clothes are ideal for sorting into same and different. (At last here is a use for all those odd socks left over from your washing!) For younger children, put odd socks on the dolls or teddies and talk about why they are odd or different in child-friendly language - 'They do not match', 'They are not the same because this one has spots and this one has lines'. Peg a different type of sock onto each of the three containers. Start with easily distinguishable socks - a long sock, a short sock, a spotty sock. For older children, use more similar socks and ask them to sort into categories such as the thick from the thin, the black from the navy blue, and so on (see also sorting in the shoe shop in 'Maths through role play', page 39).

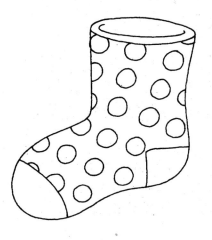

Which washing basket?

You will need:

Assortment of clothes

Washing baskets, boxes or bags

Play 'sorting out the washing into baskets'. Put a pile of clothing on the floor and use three linen or washing baskets. Label the baskets with pictures of colours or types for sorting. For younger children, begin with colour. Another time make new labels, one for socks, one for shirts and one for dresses. For older children introduce other categories such as all the adult clothes in one basket, the children's in another, the whites in another. Use baby clothes as well. Leave the activity out for children to play on their own.

Key words:

same

different

pattern

shape

match

find

sort

group

set

compare

order

Sorting by mathematical criteria (group activity)

Sorting is about matching like with like, looking for characteristics which are common to a group of objects. With younger children start by using one criterion such as colour, shape or size. For colour, use sorting hoops, trays, bowls or coloured sheets of paper. Show the children a red object. Ask the children to hunt around the room for something red. When they come back to the table, put all the red

things onto the red paper or in the red bowl or hoop. Repeat the activity with other colours. Then move on to activities such as finding something which is not red.

To sort by size take a collection of big and small of the same objects, for example buttons. Put all the small buttons into a small pot and all the big buttons into a big pot. Talk about how they decided which ones went where.

Sorting by shape can be done even if children do not know all the shape names. Put all the shapes in the middle of the table or on the floor. Show them a triangle. Ask the children to see if they can find any more shapes the same as yours. 'Can you find any more shapes that have three corners?'. 'Can you sort the tins from the boxes in the grocer's shop?'

Once they can sort into sets of same and different, extend children by combining criteria. Make up activities which involve sorting the big blue triangles from the small yellow

Assessment

Sorting

❑ Does the child explain why he is sorting?

❑ Can the child sort by a fixed criterion (all the cars)?

❑ Can the child sort by property (all the blue cars)?

❑ Can the child sort by mathematical criteria (all the big cars, all the shapes with three corners)?

❑ Can the child sort and resort using different criteria (all the blue cars and all the red cars, then all the cars with doors that open/do not open)?

❑ Can the child sort number related sets (vehicles with four wheels from things with two wheels)?

❑ Is the child aware that things can belong in more than one set? (red cars in 'things that move' and 'red cars')

---

triangles. Then move on to resort objects according to other basic criteria, dividing triangles and circles, so all the various colours are in one set. Older or more able children may put things that are common to both sets in an overlapping section of a sorting hoop. Things that do not belong in either set can be placed outside the hoop. (For example, if you had five buses, five cars and one tractor and were sorting them into groups.)

Older children should be encouraged to use mathematical language as they sort according to mathematical criteria. When using Logiblocs, assuming they can already sort shapes by colour and size, introduce the idea of thick and thin - the thick blue triangles

(regardless of size), the thin yellow circles. Make it more challenging for the older ones. Ask them, for example, to pick out all the shapes with four corners so that they can identify squares and rectangles. The older the child the more closely they should be able to notice similarities and differences.

Another activity for older children is to use pictures of faces from magazines - cut out all the eyes and ask the children to find the pairs that match. They could stick them on to a sheet of paper. You could also use pictures from magazines to make your own jigsaws which the children have to match back together again to complete.

Jigsaws - matching the pieces

Always have a range of jigsaws for varying abilities ranging from tray puzzles (where pieces match the picture on the tray) to number jigsaws and picture puzzles. Encourage older children to use the lid of the box in order to match the pieces together.

Sorting for fun

Leave out plastic bowls on the table or sorting hoops on the floor with objects for children to sort as they play independently. Commercial sets such as dinosaurs or Compare Bears are useful but everyday objects can do the same job.

Start with easily distinguishable objects. Move on to objects which are nearly the same or similar, such as shells, buttons or conkers. Children will need to look closely to sort these. Then go on to sort by number. Ask the children to put the same number of buttons in each pot or sort the buttons with two holes from those with four holes. Ask them to put the same number of cars in each line or the same number of bricks in each tower.

Tidying up time

Sorting can be reinforced in many everyday activities, particularly in tidying away equipment. Make sure all your trays, storage boxes and drawers are labelled (pictures from catalogues are useful). When children put things back where they belong they have learned to sort by category - bricks in this box, cars in that one, and so on. For older children write numerals on the containers, such as pencil pots, so they have to count in the right number of pencils.

Matching

Matching is closely related to sorting. Through matching activities children learn to compare and visually match objects. This will lead to comparing and matching numbers and shapes. Children learn to compare and match by mathematical concepts. This encourages the use of mathematical vocabulary such as 'heavy' and 'light'.

Matching involves one-to-one correspondence. As they play together children will experience matching. They will find a nappy for each doll, a cup for each child, a menu for each customer in the cafe. Matching is also connected to patterns and relationships - knife and fork, cup and saucer, laying out place settings on a table for four, matching the size of the lid to the size of the saucepan.

As they learn to count accurately they will move on to count rather than match one to one. For example, they match the number to number as they work out that five children will need five cups. Children can move on to match numerals to objects, for example the number five on a card to five bricks. In matching games such as lotto or dominoes children will progress from:

❑ matching a picture to a picture (for example shape, colour or object) to

❑ matching a number to a picture (for example two with two balls) to

❑ matching a number to a number (two with the numeral 2).

The story of 'Goldilocks and the three bears' is a simple but effective way to introduce matching and ordering by size and number. You could make props using shoe boxes and teddy bears. Provide bowls and cutlery of big, little and medium size.

Pegboards and bead threading can be used to practise matching patterns.

Maths through role play

Role play is a common feature in pre-school settings. Some Reception classes also have a home corner or life experience centre. However, the learning potential of the role-play area is not always recognised or realised and the scope for mathematical development is often lost at the expense of learning in other areas, such as language or creative development. Associating something imaginative, such as role play, with a traditionally formal subject like mathematics does not always come naturally!

Early Learning Goals

These activities will help you work towards the following goals:

❑ Say and use number names in order in familiar contexts.

❑ Count reliably up to ten everyday objects.

❑ Recognise numerals 1 to 9.

❑ Use language such as 'greater', 'smaller', 'heavier' or 'lighter' to compare quantities.

❑ Use language such as 'circle' or 'bigger' to describe the shape and size of solid and flat shapes.

❑ Use developing mathematical ideas and methods to solve practical problems.

Children need opportunities to explore, enjoy, learn, practise and talk about their understanding of number, measurement, pattern and shape. Role play can provide those opportunities. One of the goals for Mathematical Development is 'say and use number names in familiar contexts'. The role-play area can provide the familiar context a child needs to have the confidence to explore and use numbers.

Planning mathematical role play

To promote mathematics through role play, the area needs to be well planned and carefully resourced. It is best to focus on the potential learning objectives and plan the role-play area accordingly. The good thing about a role-play area is its flexibility. It can be changed according to the theme of the week, month or term. If you have been learning about 'People who help us', for example, the role-play area could be any number of settings - a hospital, doctor's surgery, optician's, vet's or school to name but a few. It can be a castle, a spaceship, a train or an aeroplane. It can be McDonalds, a garden centre or a puppet theatre. Even where space is limited, role-play activities can be promoted.

The role-play area must appeal to the children or it will not be used to the full. A post office which consists of a few pieces of paper, a dried-up felt-tip and a handful of used envelopes on a table is unlikely to attract the children's interest. A vet's with a few fluffy toy dogs will not promote much enthusiasm. However, with careful planning you can provide an appropriate, stimulating area at little expense. At the planning stage you could meet together as a staff team and brainstorm ideas for promoting mathematical development in the role-play area. Shops are ideal for developing mathematical concepts and language.

Making the most of the home corner

Many settings do not make the most of the home corner. Not only does it rarely change character but even when it is a 'home corner' the learning potential is under exploited. A limited home corner might consist of a few jumbled up clothes squashed in a box, an assorted mixture of plastic cups left over from various sets but not making a complete set, a broken dolls' cot and a pile of dirty and chewed up soft toys. By contrast you should aim for a stimulating, carefully planned and well-equipped home corner to extend learning in all areas, including mathematics. Space may be an issue but suggestions include:

❑ Matching coloured place settings of cutlery and crockery for four people

❑ Small table and four chairs

❑ Well organised dressing-up rail with various sized hats/shoes/clothing including those from other cultures

❑ Phones and phone book

❑ Recipe books

❑ Assorted pans of varying sizes with lids

❑ Dolls of various sizes

❑ Calendar, clock, noticeboard and posters on walls

❑ Play cooker, kitchen scales, play food/tins/packets

❑ Paper and pens

❑ Patterned wallpaper, curtains, tablecloths

Starting points

Although role play is primarily about allowing children to use their imaginations, they do need some starting points to build on and represent in their play. It is always a

good idea for children to observe or experience what happens in a real life version of the role-play area. The best quality role play comes when children have had direct experience beforehand. The theme may be something most children have experienced, such as a house, doctor's, shoe shop or McDonalds. If not, you could take them on a visit which is also a good opportunity to collect resources! If you are within walking distance of shops you may be able to take the group out to visit the local post office, travel agents or surgery. Prepare the children beforehand and build on their prior knowledge and experiences. If this is not possible, the ideas can be introduced on video or through pictures and books. Alternatively, a visitor may come in - for example, an optician - and give some demonstrations. It is important that the visitor is able to give clear explanations at the children's level and uses visual aids to support the talk.

A post office

Any type of shop encourages use of numbers and mathematical language provided it has been carefully planned. The choice of resources is crucial. Take the post office as an example.

You should provide as many of the things that would be found in a post office as possible. A selection of envelopes in various sizes, shapes and colours will allow children to classify according to properties. Children could have trays or tins to sort into. Sheets of writing paper in various sizes will encourage children to experiment fitting the sheets of paper into the appropriate envelope and folding it in various ways. Used birthday and Christmas cards can also be used and matched to envelopes. Children can say number names as they use numeral or date stamps to frank the

envelopes. Postage stamps serve a similar purpose. Provide a post box so that children can experiment with what will fit through the slot - they will soon realise that an envelope stuffed full of toys is too big! Borrow a postbag so the children can explore how parcels and letters fit into the bag. Children will use the weighing scales to weigh letters and parcels. The shopkeeper can then tell the customer how heavy the parcel is and how much the stamp will cost. The customer can hand over the money. Parcels of various shapes and sizes made from empty cereal boxes, for example, encourage children to describe and recognise three-dimensional shapes.

Other essential accessories in any type of shop are coins, price lists, a till and calculator, telephones and a telephone directory, all of which encourage children to work towards the Early Learning Goals associated with number. Providing other props such as a calendar and a clock will encourage children to understand and associate numbers with the concept of time.

A market stall

Visit a local greengrocers/ supermarket, farm shop or market. Real fruit and vegetables are ideal in a role-play situation. However, plastic will suffice. Set out the fruit and vegetables in baskets, boxes or trays along a table top to create the stall.

Each group of items can be labelled with a price tag from 1p to 10p (or up to 20p for older children). Ensure the weighing scales are in place. This is a good opportunity for children to explore weight in a meaningful context

Write a price list with pictures and prices for the customer to refer to. They can then be encouraged to look at the price list, point to and name the numbers they

recognise. A supply of paper (not plastic) bags in various sizes introduces problem-solving and estimating quantity. Adults can ask questions to encourage mathematical thinking and language, such as 'How many apples will go in the bag?' 'Have you got more than Lizzie or less than Lizzie?' 'Do you think your bag is heavier or lighter than mine?' 'Will everything fit into your trolley?' Customers will also use numbers and mathematical vocabulary as they ask for 'two apples' or 'May I have some more?' They will be comparing numbers by saying 'I've got two more than you'.

Children could write numbers on old cheque books, and stall holders could have a receipt pad to write on.

A major learning factor in this role-play scenario is the opportunity to sort and count everyday objects into sets. The language of early addition and subtraction can also be introduced as the children play here. Children serving will have to pick from the baskets whatever the customers order, for example, two lemons and one orange. An adult could ask 'How many pieces of fruit have you bought altogether?' When tidying up the children will sort the fruit into the right basket.

Adults can extend learning by sharing in the role play, sensitively prompting and questioning children as they play, or modelling the role of the customer or stall holder.

A shoe shop

A shoe shop is ideally suited to promote a number of the Early Learning Goals for Mathematical Development. Children will 'say and use number names' and 'recognise numerals 1 to 9' as they look at the shoe sizes. They can order numbers as they order the shoes by size. They will use language of comparison such as 'bigger than' when comparing the sizes

of the shoes. Matching will be encouraged as they find the 'other' shoe of a pair. Older children can be encouraged to count the shoes in twos. If you provide a wide range of shoes they will be able to count and sort into sets organised by size or type:

❑ size;

❑ trainers;

❑ slippers;

❑ buckles;

❑ laces;

❑ ladies';

❑ men's;

❑ children's.

A foot measure or tape measures will encourage children to recognise and use number in a meaningful context. They will enjoy playing matching games with the shoes. You could mix all the shoes up and take one out then see if they can find the matching shoe. They will explore problems as they discover what happens when a shoe is the wrong size. You can ask children questions such as 'Do you think these shoes will fit me?', 'Are they too big?', 'How much are these shoes?', 'Have you any blue slippers, size eight please?'

A pot of tea for two

The cafe or tea shop is another popular venue for young shoppers. Even an overtly simple task such as laying the table for four involves a whole range of mathematics. Children will learn about sequencing, size and patterns as they set out the plates, cups and cutlery. They will need to match on a one-to-one basis to make sure everyone has one of each. If cooking, they can weigh ingredients, match saucepan lids by size and talk about capacity and quantity as they cook and serve the food. They will order from a menu or price list. Patterns on aprons, tablecloths and tea towels can be

Assessment

Look for the child's spontaneous use of mathematical knowledge and vocabulary during role-play experiences.

talked about. Adults will no doubt be invited to join in the fun and be served endless cups of tea! They could ask for 'Two sugars and three biscuits, please'. But don't forget to pay the bill or you may end up washing up!

All these principles can be applied to other role-play shops such as:

❑ supermarket;

❑ travel agents;

❑ haberdashery;

❑ bakery;

❑ butchers;

❑ newsagents;

❑ garden centre.

Remember, role play does not depend on expensive resources and should be encouraged in early years settings even with limited space. Children's imaginations will do most of the work: indoors or outdoors, a line of chairs becomes a train or a bus, boxes become boats; a climbing frame becomes a pirate ship, a slide with a silver foil roof becomes a spaceship, a table with a blanket over the top becomes a tent. Mathematics is only one area of learning and role play has benefits across the whole early years curriculum. Children want to learn and explore mathematical ideas in this way. They will have the final word, 'Come on! Let's play shops!'

Your number's up!

The Early Learning Goals for Mathematical Development state that children are expected to 'recognise numerals 1 to 9' by the end of the reception year. Children will only learn to recognise numerals if they are exposed to them in a variety of contexts.

It is the numerals 0-9 that form the foundation for recognising all the numbers in our number system. Children will already be exposed to numerals in their daily lives, at home on videos, clocks and cookers. In the wider environment they will see car registration plates, speed limit signs, shop opening times, post box collection times, and so on. They will remember those which have some personal significance to them such as their own age, shoe size or house number. These experiences can be extended by providing a number rich environment in the nursery or reception class. Resources should include:

❑ a number frieze/line/track (at child's level);

❑ calculators;

❑ wooden and plastic numerals;

❑ magnetic numerals;

❑ telephones;

❑ numerals on containers;

❑ signs, for example '4 in the sand';

❑ numerals painted on outdoor play area;

❑ clocks;

❑ a height chart.

There are many purposes for recognising and using numerals. Four basic types and functions of numerals are:

❑ cardinal numbers: to indicate an amount or number of items;

❑ nominal numbers: to 'label' such as buses, birthday cards;

❑ ordinal numbers: to identify a position in a sequence such as house numbers or page numbers;

❑ to record measurement such as time, distance, weight.

Of course, there is no point in recognising the numeral if it means nothing. In the Foundation Stage it is important that children learn to link numerals with amounts or 'how many'. They need to know from an early stage that the numeral represents or symbolises a given number of objects. In other words, each number stands for an amount. However, they also need to understand that the amount is independent of the type of object being referred to - five apples, five bananas or five oranges have the same numeral. They are all sets of five.

Numerals are abstract and can be confusing. For example, a number six on a door does not mean that there are six people inside the house, but number six on a scissors pot may well mean that there should be six pairs of scissors in the pot (or is the pot for table number six?)!

In the same way as they learn to recognise initial letters children will

learn to recognise numerals in context. With regular practice and experience children will learn to 'read' numbers. Remember, it is much more important for children to become familiar with written numerals than to record the numbers themselves at the early stage. Recording will be easier if they have plenty of practice in touching and reading numerals. It is important that children become familiar with the shape of the numeral, so encourage them to handle the numeral or trace its shape with their finger.

Number recognition activities

A set or several sets of numeral cards or tiles is essential. When doing number rhymes, for example, children can actively participate and hold up the appropriate number of currant buns or speckled frogs. You could also make number lines on a strip of card. These can be taped to the tables for children to look at and talk about at snack time. Older children can use them for 'counting on' and 'counting back'. Many popular games such as bingo or snap can be adapted to encourage number recognition.

Who's got my number? (a small group activity)

Ask the children to pick a number from the pile of numeral cards. Talk about the numerals and ask questions. Ask 'Who has number one?', 'Who has number two?', and so on. Help them order themselves in a circle and count around the group, pointing to the numerals one at a time as you say the number. Ask who has number one, who has the next number, and so on. The children can then swap cards and you can do it all over again! They should gradually start to be able to order themselves with less and less support. At first you might put some dots on the cards for the children to count and work out the numeral but eventually remove the dots and leave only the numeral. Point out the difference between six (6) and nine (9). Use various versions of number four.

With younger children lay the cards on the table and say 'Who can see a number three?' 'Can you find the number that shows how old you are?' 'Pick up the number that shows how many fingers you have.' 'Who's got the number after this one?' As a follow-up they could make their own books of numbers or collages of numerals cut from magazines or birthday cards.

Number line (a large group activity)

This sort of activity can be done at any time, for example at register time or while waiting for drinks. You will need a long piece of string as a washing line with numeral cards folded over and hanging or pegged onto the line. At first, just put them in order and get the children to count along the line with you pointing to each numeral. Start with one to five and add more numbers as they become more experienced. Gradually begin to play games with the numbers. Each day put one in the wrong place and challenge the children to solve the problem. 'Oh no! Someone's put the number in the wrong place on our line! Which number can you see is not in the right place? Shall we count?' Then choose a child to come out and

move the number to the correct place. Choose different numbers each day. Then remove a number completely and challenge the children again. 'Which number is missing?' 'Who can hang it back in the right place?' When using more numbers you could remove two or three from the line. Leave the line accessible for children to play with independently.

Number displays

Have a 'number of the week' each week. Display the relevant numeral somewhere prominent and ask the children, 'Who can tell me the name of this week's special number?' You can then plan a range of activities around that number. If it were three, for example, you could tell stories with three in the title, set the table in the

home corner for three people, ask children to line up in threes and make biscuits the shape of number three. You could put the numeral above a display of things associated with three. This might include the story of the three pigs, sets of objects such as three dolls, a birthday card with 'three years old' on it, three toy cars, photos with three people in, a wooden number three, and so on.

Other useful ways of encouraging number recognition include reading stories, labels and recipes involving numbers. Make sure the role-play area is equipped with price lists, coins, calculators and telephones. Provide a range of number jigsaw puzzles and games. Outdoors, jump on to numbers, throw bean bags along a number track and say what number it lands on. Play games with numbered skittles. Practice makes perfect.

Assessment

Check if the child:

❑ can distinguish numbers from letters;

❑ knows the number name;

❑ can recognise the number;

❑ can read the number in a variety of contexts;

❑ can understand the numeral (can indicate how many things there are, for example there are four children allowed in the sand).

Promoting mathematical language

'For many young children mathematics has been reduced to remembering number bonds and multiplication tables and practising basic computation' (Thumpston, 1994)

The message here is that mathematics tends to focus too narrowly on number operations or 'numeracy' at the expense of other aspects such as problem-solving and the use of mathematical language. As a result, children are left with a view that maths is only about 'doing sums'. However, children need to use mathematical language to describe shape, position, size and quantity. It is essential to introduce and consolidate children's understanding of a whole range of mathematical vocabulary in planned practical activities and independent play situations. The potential of mathematical language to contribute to other areas of learning should also not be underestimated.

Children's mathematical ideas develop alongside an increasing awareness of language. Young children often take things literally. If you ask a quiet child, 'Where's your tongue?', he may put his tongue out to show you it! When you say to a child 'Find a space!', they often walk around the room. On questioning you discover that they do not understand the concept of space and are looking for a 'a space'.

The precise meaning of a word used in mathematics may be different from the child's understanding of that word in an everyday situation. Cutting a cake in half may not be an exact half in the mathematical sense. Children need to take time in learning the language of mathematics.

For most young children the first step in solving a problem is to try and verbalise it in everyday language that

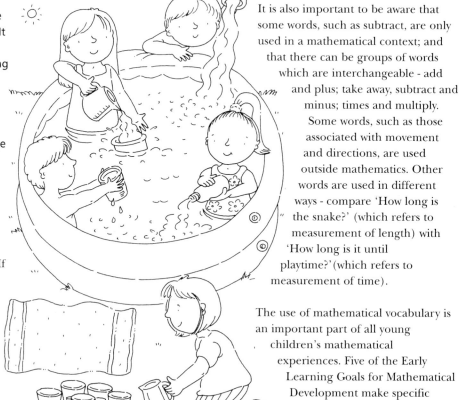

makes sense to them. The adult needs to respond in the same language and then begin to add examples of mathematical terms. For example, if a child says 'Look, my tower is bigger than yours', you could say, 'Yes, it's taller isn't it?' The child can then build on his existing store of words such as 'share', 'times', 'take away' and 'same' to develop strategies which help him to grasp the meaning of more formal equivalents such as 'divide', 'multiply', 'subtract' and 'equals'.

It is also important to be aware that some words, such as subtract, are only used in a mathematical context; and that there can be groups of words which are interchangeable - add and plus; take away, subtract and minus; times and multiply. Some words, such as those associated with movement and directions, are used outside mathematics. Other words are used in different ways - compare 'How long is the snake?' (which refers to measurement of length) with 'How long is it until playtime?' (which refers to measurement of time).

The use of mathematical vocabulary is an important part of all young children's mathematical experiences. Five of the Early Learning Goals for Mathematical Development make specific reference to mathematical language. The goals state that by the end of the Foundation Stage, most children will be able to:

❑ Use language such as 'more' or 'less' to compare two numbers.

❑ Use language such as 'greater', 'smaller', 'heavier' or 'lighter' to compare quantities.

❑ Use language such as 'circle' or 'bigger' to describe the shape and size of solid and flat shapes.

❑ In practical activities and discussion begin to use the vocabulary involved in adding and subtracting.

❑ Use everyday words to describe position.

The first four of these have been referred to extensively elsewhere in this book and are mentioned again here. The fifth is discussed below. Adult intervention will take the form

of sensitively and knowledgeably planning and participating in activities, providing, for example, the names of plane and solid shapes or using the language of position. The use of everyday words in relation to positions in space can be promoted in practical contexts. Examples of positional language include:

up/down

in front/behind

above/on top

inside/outside

over/under/below

through

top/bottom

next to/beside

before/after

opposite

between

Early Learning Goals

These activities will help you work towards the following goals:

❑ Use language such as 'greater', 'smaller', 'heavier' or 'lighter' to compare quantities.

❑ In practical activities and discussion begin to use the vocabulary involved in adding and subtracting.

❑ Use language such as 'circle' or 'bigger' to describe the shape and size of solid and flat shapes.

❑ Use everyday words to describe position.

❑ Use developing mathematical ideas and methods to solve practical problems.

Starting points

A good starting point is to listen to and talk about position using books, pictures and stories such as *Where's Spot?* or the *Bear Hunt* story. Children love to act this out and join in the words. When looking at other pictures in stories ask the children questions such as:

❑ Is the frog under the rock?

❑ Who is next to the frog?

❑ What can you see on top of the table?

❑ Who is behind the gingerbread man?

❑ What is beside the wardrobe?

make a basic obstacle course

You will need:

Balancing beam, bench or plank

Slide

Straight line (taped, painted or drawn)

Tunnel (or table with blanket over the top)

Cones

Something to walk around (for example a post or a tree)

Safety mat or soft surface

An obstacle course is an ideal opportunity for children to listen to and use mathematical language in a meaningful context. It includes the language of movement and direction. The following passage gives examples of the language opportunities in a basic, straightforward obstacle course, but can be adapted and extended according to your resources and layout:

What Learning Looks Like... 43

Walk **forwards** on the **straight line** to the slide. Climb **up** the steps to the top.

Look **in front** of you to make sure it's safe. Slide **down** to the bottom.

Walk **backwards along** the bench. Use your arms to **balance**. **Turn** around and jump **off** the end.

Now crawl **through** the tunnel.

Jump **up and down** all the way to the **corner**.

Walk **across** the grass **curving in** and **out** of the cones.

Make sure you stay one **behind** the other.

Go **around** the tree and stop **behind** the yellow line.

The key point is for children to have a wide experience in using language in a variety of relevant situations. This will develop confidence and ultimately more use of language.

Small world play

Adults can join children's small world play and use mathematical language in discussion and questions. Road and rail layouts, zoos, garages and so on all offer valuable opportunities to use positional language. 'Is the doll in the highchair under the bed?' 'Who is behind the kitchen door?'

A small group structured activity with farm animals can be used to assess children's understanding.

You will need:

Sets of four different farm animals (sheep, cows, pigs, horses)

Various surfaces to represent fields

Arrange the sets of animals in the fields. Set children little tasks as if playing a game. Say 'I'm going to tell you where to put the animals and I want you to listen to what I say and move them wherever I tell you'. Then give a variety of tasks, one at a time, observing closely and prompting children where necessary.

Sample tasks:

'Take a pig and put it next to a cow.'

'Take a horse and put it behind a sheep.'

'Take a sheep and put it in front of a pig.'

'Put all the sheep in a circle.'

'Put one horse in each corner of the field.'

Quicker learners may be able to take turns to tell the rest of the group what to do.

Alternatively, you could make up a story about the animals and get the children to move them at the appropriate points. It might be something like this, but you could improvise as you go along:

Once upon a time there was a farmer. His animals were in four fields. One night he went to bed. When he woke up the next morning, he had a shock! They had all moved into the wrong place! The sheep were behind the cows; the horses were next to the pigs. The farmer jumped out of bed and shouted at the sheep. 'Sheep, walk forward into your field. And the pigs walked forwards. Horses - jump over the fence and go back into your field. And the horses jumped over the fence ...

Assessment activities

How do you assess children's use of mathematical language? It is not straightforward and has to be based on close, sometimes time-consuming observations and through asking questions which encourage children to think and talk about their ideas and experiences. Formal testing and assessment is not an appropriate way to assess this aspect. Activities such as the following are more revealing:

❑ Take a pile of 20 (sweets or buttons).

❑ Divide it into two unequal sets - one each.

❑ Ask the child, 'Who do you think has more?'

This will tell you whether the child has understood the language of comparison and knows that more can mean a larger quantity.

❑ Take two objects.

❑ Let the child hold them, one in each hand.

❑ Ask the child, 'Which is the heaviest?' or 'Which is lighter?'

This will tell you whether or not the child understands the meaning of heavy and light.

More formal terms such as grammes, litres, centimetres and so on are less important at this stage but can be introduced in context, such as during cookery sessions. As they build vertically or horizontally with interlocking construction equipment or block play they will often make comparisons trying to build something 'taller' or 'longer' than themselves.

Extending children's mathematical language will make a significant contribution to their communication skills. But it can be confusing even for adults - what is a triangular prism? Some adults are also confused about general terms such as capacity - the maximum amount a vessel can contain

More mathematical vocabulary	
same	different
full	empty
heavy	light
thick	thin
long	short
tall	small
wide	narrow
balances	

- and volume - the bulk, size or dimension of something.

It is important for adults to be clear and not to pass on incorrect information to children. For example, telling them that a cube is a square or that a ball is a circle when it is really a sphere. Remember, the more interesting, enjoyable and meaningful the mathematics is to the children the more they will learn.

Mathematical Development

Addition and subtraction

When the words addition and subtraction first appeared in the Desirable Learning Outcomes document, many providers of early years education were aghast at the thought of having to 'teach' three-year-olds how to add and subtract. To an extent, the outcome was misinterpreted and the intention was to maximise opportunities for simple addition and subtraction, for example in daily routines or in singing number rhymes. Many children even as young as three can understand adding and subtracting providing the ideas are introduced in a developmentally appropriate way, in other words in a relevant and practical context. Three of the Early Learning Goals are related to adding and subtracting:

❑ In practical activities and discussion begin to use the vocabulary involved in adding and subtracting.

❑ Find one more or one less than a number from one to ten.

❑ Begin to relate addition to combining two groups of objects and subtraction to 'taking away'.

Remember these are expected outcomes by the end of the Reception year or as the child is about to start Year 1. The use of the word 'begin' in two of these goals is especially relevant. There is no suggestion that we rush out and buy addition and subtraction worksheets or teach children to do 'sums'. Formal recording would be totally premature at this stage. Instead the goals which mention adding and

subtracting need to be seen as an expectation that children will be provided with a gentle and gradual introduction to addition and subtraction. The implication is that children's early experiences will be practical and involve plenty of discussion. In this way children will be prepared more readily for the more formal calculations they encounter later on. At this stage children will invent their own ways of doing addition and subtraction, for example by drawing little sticks or using their fingers.

The language

Various words are used to talk about addition such as 'altogether', 'makes' and 'more'. More formal terms such as

'add' and 'total' come later on. It is important to use child-friendly language from the beginning. The important concept for the children is that two groups of objects can be added together to make a new number, which is more than the first number (except when using zero). Children often combine objects during their spontaneous play and it is adult questioning and modelling which will help them begin to understand the processes involved. Take a group of children playing with the toy cars and the garage. One child parks two red cars another brings a third blue car and puts it next to the other two cars. When asked how many cars there are altogether they will count to three. The adult could then say something like, 'Yes, two red ones and one blue one - that makes three altogether. Well done'.

Early Learning Goals

These activities will help you work towards the following goals:

❑ In practical activities and discussion begin to use the vocabulary involved in adding and subtracting.

❑ Use language such as 'more' or 'less' to compare two numbers.

❑ Find one more or one less than a number from one to ten.

❑ Begin to relate addition to combining two groups of objects and subtraction to 'taking away'.

You could join in the play with the train set. Children enjoy taking the carriages apart and then putting them back on again. Here they are exploring the ideas of adding and taking away. They are realising that when they take carriages off the train becomes shorter and when they put them back on they are adding more carriages. Simple questions such as 'How many carriages have you got left now?' will help children use the language associated with adding and taking away.

Scoring games are a good introduction to combining numbers or groups of objects. If a child rolls a ball and knocks down two skittles on his first turn, then on his second attempt he knocks down another, ask the other children to say what is happening. At first children need to count and recount to find out how many there are in total but with practice they will soon recall that two and two more are always four. Other opportunities will occur in the daily routine. There are six boys and three girls - how many children are there altogether? In familiar number rhymes, songs and stories more are often added or taken away. Start with small numbers such as 'Two little dicky birds' and progress to higher numbers when the children begin to show they have grasped the idea.

Once children begin to understand that addition is related to combining and subtraction to taking away a number of objects from a group, move on to consolidate and assess using coloured Unifix cubes. Play a game where children build towers according to your instructions, for example 'Three red and four blue makes seven altogether'. Take away the red ones. Can the children predict how many they will have left?

Number lines

For finding one more or less than a given number children need to be able to count reliably forwards and backwards. Number lines and friezes are useful here for children to count 'back' and 'forwards' along the number line. They need to be asked and to predict, 'What comes after five?' or 'What comes before six?' They need to be secure in ordering numbers before moving on to the idea of 'one more'. Once they can order the numbers and count reliably from one to ten everyday objects they need to understand the meaning of the words 'more' or 'less'. Children often know what number comes after their age. They will say 'I'm three now but soon I'm going to be "this many" ' (holding up four fingers) or say the number four.

Cooking is also an excellent way to practise using the language of addition and subtraction. How many spoonfuls of sugar altogether? Now how many more spoonfuls do we need? We need ten cakes and ate three. How many are left?

The following activity is adapted from the national numeracy project and is aimed at Reception aged children in the spring term.

The dish and the spoon

Learning objective: to explore 'more' and 'fewer'.

> You will need:
>
> Dishes and spoons
>
> Cubes

Introduce the activity by showing the children a number of dishes (three) and spoons (six). Ask, 'Are there more dishes or more spoons?' Listen to their responses and then say the answer yourself using the words 'more' and 'fewer'. You could say: 'There are more spoons than dishes.' 'There are fewer dishes than spoons.' Encourage the children to match the spoons and dishes in order to show that there are more spoons. Talk to the children as they explore. Ask 'How many spoons are there?' 'How many dishes are there?' Encourage them to discover how they could make the number of spoons and dishes correspond. They will realise they need more dishes. Ask 'What can we do to make the same number of dishes and spoons?' Either they can add three more dishes or they can take away three spoons. Repeat this type of activity several times using different objects such as knives and forks, cups and saucers.

Assessment

Does the child:

❑ add one or two in a number rhyme or scoring game?

❑ talk about how many altogether and how many are left?

❑ solve simple problems using addition and/or subtraction?

Associated language:

number names one to ten

number

count

take away

same

equal

as many as

more than

fewer than

add

same number as

How many more?

match

altogether

Problem-solving

Problem-solving requires children to use logical thinking and apply mathematical skills in a practical situation. Children who are confident with small numbers may begin to use these to solve simple practical problems. The early years setting should provide experiences that encourage children to:

❏ talk about predictions;

❏ plan ways or methods;

❏ give explanations.

Problems when playing

The main ways in which children encounter problem-solving situations are in their own play or in the daily routine. You might observe them creating and solving their own mathematical problems, for example as they try to work out how to make a bridge which is high enough for the trains to pass under. Watch as they puzzle over how to make pieces of train track fit together to make a figure of eight. Eventually they either get frustrated and walk away (unless there is a sensitive adult nearby to offer support) or they work it out. If they do solve the problem they often come and ask an adult to have a look. Although not consciously thinking 'Oh, I've solved a problem', they realise that they have achieved a solution.

In playing with a garage and road mat, for example, they might have to work out how to fit a certain number of cars in the parking space by counting the spaces and then the cars or by matching one to one. They may try to fit too many cars in the lift or put too many down the ramp at once. In this way they need to make choices or decisions as to the next step.

Construction and creative play are excellent ways of promoting problem-solving. As they design and build children will ask themselves questions such as 'How can I stop this wall from toppling over?' or 'How can I make a roof for this house?' If there are not enough large bricks, do they decide to use two small bricks instead of one large one? Playing with construction equipment which joins together also helps children work out and plan what to do. If one piece won't join on to another shall I turn it round? Duplo, Mobilo and Lego bricks are ideal resources for problem-solving.

Observe, listen and question

It is important for adults to observe children closely and listen to their questions or comments.

Jennie: 'I can't make this doll fit in this pram.'

Adult: 'Why won't it fit?'

Jennie: 'It's too big.'

Adult: 'What can you do then?'

Jennie: 'I'll take the pillows and blankets out.'

Try to ask open-ended questions which make the children think about one or more solutions. 'What else do you think you could try?' In the above scenario, Jennie may have said she would try a bigger pram or a smaller doll. Similar situations occur when children can't fit all the shopping in the toy trolley or put so much plastic food on a plate that it falls off.

Planned problems

Certain events or activities can be planned to encourage children to think mathematically in order to solve practical problems. If you were doing a topic on 'Seasons' and talking about holidays, for example, you could organise a group activity which involved packing a pile of clothes and other items into a suitcase, rucksack or backpack. Even adults find fitting everything into their suitcase a problem and have to take it out to rearrange it until it fits in properly!

Another way of challenging children to try out different plans and methods is to design (verbally) and build a model. It can be really simple, such as when a child suggests, 'Let's make a bus!'. Challenge them to think mathematically by asking questions such as 'How many passengers will there be?' 'How many chairs do we need?' 'What can we use for a steering wheel?' 'What else do we need?' 'Where will the driver sit?' 'How many wheels do we need?' 'What could we make the wheels from?'

More complicated designing and making activities include building a model plane. 'What could you build it with?' 'How high will it be?' 'How wide?' 'How will we make wings?' 'Will it have wheels?'

Other problems relate more directly to number. Some of these include:

❑ There are four people on the bus. Two more get on. How many are there altogether?

❑ The bus is full - there are only six seats. How can we let Ben get on?

❑ If two more get on, how many people will there be?

They may also involve using mathematical equipment such as the weighing scales to see if a parcel is heavy or light or exploring how the marbles can be organised to balance the scales. You could put a number of objects in a box and tell the children how many you have put in. Let them take one out and say how many they think are left in the box, even though they cannot see them.

Teddy bears' picnic

Involve the children in planning a summer picnic. 'How many children will there be altogether?' 'How will they know when and how to come?' 'Will it be in the morning or afternoon?' 'What time will it start/finish?' 'Where will it be?' 'How will you make sure the teddies don't get mixed up?' 'What food will you need?' 'What else will you need?' 'What will you do if it rains?' 'Where will people sit?'

Involving the children in decisions such as these will lead to a variety of mathematical ideas and explanations. The children will have to think logically and talk about what is and isn't practical. Activities stemming from this one idea might include the following:

❑ counting children

❑ planning a room layout

❑ counting tables and chairs

❑ deciding where the teddies will sit

❑ discussion about time, sequence of events

❑ working out numbers of bowls, straws, cups, and so on

❑ choosing the right size tablecloths for tables

❑ laying the tables correctly, matching cups/plates

❑ making cakes and sandwiches

❑ sharing out biscuits, cakes, crisps

❑ pouring drinks

❑ tidying up/sorting

The aspects of mathematics involved in problem-solving often incorporate:

❑ measurement

❑ counting

❑ classifying

Early Learning Goals

❑ Use developing mathematical ideas and methods to solve practical problems.

❑ shape sorting

❑ adding and subtracting

❑ estimating

The final word in this section goes to Ofsted. A report, *The Quality of Education in Nursery Voucher Settings* (1997) concluded that: 'the great majority of institutions teach children to recognise and write numbers and to count, recognise mathematical shapes and use simple mathematical terms to describe shape, position, size and quantities. The main weakness is the lack of attention to problem-solving skills involving, for example, simple transactions with money .... and activities involving simple addition and subtraction problems.'

With careful planning by early years workers this situation can soon be remedied.

Assessment

Assessment is mainly through close observation of the children as they play or take part in planned activities.

❑ Do they ask questions?

❑ Do they give explanations?

❑ Can they predict what might happen if ...?

❑ Do they consider or try alternatives?

❑ Do they find solutions?

Seasons

Maths for all seasons

Children will already have begun to develop a sense of time as they experience everyday routines and recognise recurring daily, weekly and seasonal patterns, such as summer holidays or Christmas. Each of the seasons has opportunities to offer in certain aspects of Mathematical Development. This can be done by incorporating mathematical activities into the separate themes of 'Summer', 'Autumn', 'Spring' and 'Winter', either as a part of an overall topic on 'Seasons' or as four individual mini-topics throughout the year.

Starting points

In talking about the seasons it is important to introduce the concept of change. As the year progresses, changes happen in the environment. The most familiar to the children will be changes in the weather. They will probably already associate hot with summer and cold with winter. In the 'Summer' or 'Winter' topic you could incorporate an activity based on sorting and matching opposites.

Sorting activity

You will need:

Various objects associated with summer and winter

Sorting hoops

Put all the items in a large box or bin. Ask the children to take turns to pick an item out of the box. Talk about what it is and see if they can decide

whether it belongs in the summer or winter hoop. For the older children this could be extended to include items which belong in both or neither hoop.

Examples of items which belong in the summer hoop:

ice cream cone; holiday brochure;

postcard; T-shirt; bucket and spade; thin socks; sandals; picnic items; summer holiday photos.

Examples of items which belong in the winter hoop:

scarf; gloves; thick socks; winter holiday brochure; soup tin; hot chocolate packet; de-icer; boots;

Early Learning Goals

❏ Count reliably up to ten everyday objects.

❏ Use language such as 'greater', 'smaller', 'heavier' or 'lighter' to compare quantities.

❏ Use language such as 'circle' or 'bigger' to describe the shape and size of solid and flat shapes.

flask; photos of snow; Christmas tree decoration; Christmas card.

Items which could go at the intersection between both hoops:

swimming trunks; book; newspaper; map; passport.

Spring

Spring is the time for growth and change. Opportunities for mathematical learning occur related to these two themes. Firstly, spring is a time when most nurseries and infant classrooms plant seeds and watch them grow. Popular choices are cress seed, crocus bulbs and broad beans. These activities cross the whole curriculum but can easily be adapted to draw on some of the mathematical concepts in the Early Learning Goals. You will need seeds, soil, plant pots (parents may provide these) and small garden tools. Each child should be allowed to plant his or her own seed or seeds. Opportunities will occur to count bulbs as they begin to flower, to count petals on daffodils, and to measure and record growth. Young children can measure using strips of paper and mark the height of the flower on the strip. Older children may be able to count centimetres. If you grow daffodils children could order them according to height. Encourage the language of comparison - 'Which

daffodil is the tallest?' 'If they are laid flat, which has the longest stem?' Look for patterns in the leaves and petals.

You could link this number rhyme in with the theme of growing:

Five little peas in a pea pod pressed (children crouch down on ground)

One grew, two grew and so did all the rest (children slowly stretch up half-way tall)

They grew and they grew (children slowly stretch up a bit more)

And they could not stop (children stretch as tall as possible)

And all of a sudden one went POP!

Four little peas ...

Make a display of 'Mary, Mary, quite contrary' with numerals to match the various flowers growing in the garden. Displays and activities based on stories such as 'Jack and the beanstalk' and 'The ugly duckling' also link well with this topic.

Soil play

Put soil or compost in the sand tray and provide a range of different sized plastic plant pots, sieves and spades, and some pairs of gardening gloves. Children can then explore how much soil the pots hold. They can use mathematical language as they empty and fill the pots. They can order the plant pots according to size and sort out those which are empty from those which are full.

The farm - a matching activity

Many groups take their children out on a farm trip during the spring term to see the young animals. This is an excellent way to introduce a matching the adult to its young activity.

You will need:

Set of small world farm animals

or

Pictures of familiar farm animals

Sheep - lamb

Horse - foal

Cow - calf

Paper

Glue

You could do this with the toy farm animals or as a cutting and sticking activity. Talk about each adult animal in turn and then about each baby. 'Who knows what this animal is called?' 'Is it big or little?' 'Is it the mother or the baby?' Let the children take turns to choose an animal and then find the matching baby. Even if they can't remember the names, the mathematical learning is the matching of adult and its offspring . Sing 'Old MacDonald had a farm' and substitute calf for cow and so on. If using cut-out pictures, children could place the adult animals on one side and the

to sort all the horses (young and old) from all the cows. They could sort and order the farm animals by size or count the number of legs.

Set up the role-play area as a farm shop. This will offer a whole range of mathematical experiences (see 'Maths through role play', pages 36-39).

Sequencing

Children can be introduced to sequencing when talking about life-cycles. The story of the hungry caterpillar or the life-cycle of a frog are

Sand and water play are ideal for introducing mathematical language and should be a permanent part of any setting throughout the year but perhaps more so outside in the summer.

Try out different sports activities. Set up a mini-tennis tournament using bats and balls and keeping score up to five or ten. Younger children who cannot record numerals can make a tally mark on a board. The 'Summer' topic lends itself to a whole range of games involving scoring and counting. These include mini-golf and skittles.

Summer is also the ideal time for a treasure hunt. Give children a pictorial set of things to find such as one big yellow triangle or three red buttons, four blades of grass, five leaves, and so on.

On the theme of travel and holidays you could design and make an aeroplane, bus or train for travelling on holiday. Let the children join in the processes of designing and making. They will have to help make decisions. 'How many passengers are you going to have?' 'How many chairs will you need?' 'How many windows?' 'How many doors?' 'What shape will the doors be?'

matching young on the other, saying what they are doing as they go along. Younger children could begin just matching big and little: a big rabbit, a little rabbit.

The theme can be developed as it progresses to incorporate counting and sorting activities. For example, 'How many piglets can you see?' 'How many calves?' 'Which animal has the most babies?' You could get children

good starting points. There are a number of books and jigsaw puzzles available to support these activities.

Summer

The most obvious resource for mathematics in the summer is the outdoor area. Talk to the children about things that people do in the summer, such as outdoor sports and activities or holidays.

The role-play area could be set up as a travel agents. Provide a variety of brochures, maps, tickets, old cheque books, coins, a phone, till and calculator. Children will gain mathematical experiences as they weigh luggage, take money for holidays, write tickets, check passport numbers, count numbers of passengers and so on. They will talk to each other about time of leaving and arriving. What time does the boat leave? They will encounter numerals in the brochures.

Shells

Shells are an excellent resource for the mathematical Early Learning Goals. A variety of activities can be planned including using shells as the focus for simple practice in counting one to five. For a group of young children, hide some shells in a shallow tray of sand. Let them take turns at finding one shell then another. Ask 'How many shells have you got now?' Younger children also enjoy weighing shells on the balancing scales.

For older or more able children, shells are a good resource for classifying or sorting into groups. Many are similar and children need good discriminatory skills to sort them by size, colour or pattern. Your older children should be able to explain why they are choosing some shells as distinct from others. Use a magnifying glass to look at the patterns and shapes. Older or more able children could play the 'shell in the sand game' as well but extend the questioning to focus on addition and subtraction as well as counting to higher numbers. Give each child five shells. Put two in the sand. 'How many have you got left?' Then move on to more complex questioning.

Autumn

A good mathematical theme for autumn is 'Food', especially as it is harvest time. Younger children could sort and weigh various fruits and vegetables by kind. Older children could classify foods into groups of fruits, vegetables and cereals. Fruit can be cut into halves or quarters for break time. Tins and bottles in all shapes and sizes can be ordered by size. Making bread or soup and all the weighing and measuring that go with cooking are essential parts of this topic. Other aspects of autumn include looking for patterns in leaves and sorting the leaves into groups, making scarecrow models, and

counting how many apples children can bob in a bowl of water. Children could divide conkers into sets by size or texture.

Winter

There are many spontaneous opportunities for sorting and counting related to winter. Look at Christmas tree decorations with the children and sort them by type: those that are balls, those made of wood, paper and so on. Children could investigate patterns as they make their own Christmas decorations or use paper folding and cutting to make snowflakes. Winter clothes such as scarves, socks, gloves and jumpers usually have patterns to be explored.

These are just a few ideas of how Mathematical Development can be incorporated into seasonal activities. Other festivals and celebrations such as Chinese New Year could also be used in similar ways. Why not turn your role-play area into a Chinese restaurant and see?

Assessment

Can the child:

❏ talk about the weather?

❏ sort clothes into summer and winter?

❏ talk about the pictures on a seasonal calendar?

❏ sequence a pattern of events, for example say what happens next in the nursery/school day?

❏ distinguish today, tonight, tomorrow and yesterday?

Resources

Planning for Learning through Spring; Summer; Autumn and *Winter*: a series of books from Step Forward Publishing. *Seasons* poster pack also available.

Ten green bottles

From an early age children begin to explore mathematical concepts as they play with bath toys, and help with the washing-up. Water tray activities are an essential part of a water topic in any early years setting. Water play is particularly relevant in the aspects of Mathematical Development that relate to exploring capacity and using mathematical language.

A water tray should be available on a regular basis for all young children. However, many settings offer water play on a limited basis. Sometimes this is because the children tend to make a mess, or it takes too long to fill and empty the tray. Some groups only offer water play outside in the summer months which means skills cannot be built up progressively.

However, with a little thought, water play experiences can be provided. Why not use a washing-up bowl or bucket on a plastic mat? The more the children become used to playing in the water tray the less mess they make. Water play does need adult support if children are to learn to use and understand the mathematical language involved. They also need the opportunity to consolidate and practise what they have learned through playing and experimenting independently. It needs to be organised in small groups with clear rules as to how many children are allowed in the water at any one time.

Of course, simply having a water tray is not enough. To explore the potential for Mathematical Development in the water tray you also need to provide a range of resources. These include:

Early Learning Goals

❑ Recognise numerals 1 to 9

❑ Use language such as 'greater', 'smaller', 'heavier' or 'lighter' to compare quantities.

❑ Use everyday words to describe position.

❑ Use developing mathematical ideas and methods to solve practical problems.

Cups, pots, bottles, jugs and containers in different shapes and sizes

Sieves

Funnels

Plastic teaspoons

Spoons

Tubing

Sponges

Straws

Sponges

Objects which float and sink

Plastic coloured boats

Starting point

A popular starting point is the song 'Ten green bottles' which be extended to include numeral recognition, ordering, counting and subtracting.

You will need:

Ten plastic bottles (same size and capacity)

Green food colouring

Water

Numeral cards

Colour some water green and put the same amount in each bottle. Attach a numeral card, for example by tying it on the neck of each bottle. Choose children to hold each bottle and sit down as they 'fall off the wall'. Each time one 'falls', ask the children, 'How many are left?' Emphasise that one has fallen. This song really helps children achieve the goal of 'find one more or one less than a number from one to ten'.

Younger children could work with five bottles. Older children may manage counting back in twos. Change the words and sing 'If two green bottles should accidentally fall' each time. Another time vary the amount of water in each bottle. Take the numeral cards off. Stand them in a random order and see if the children can order the bottles from the one which holds the most to the one which holds the least. Introduce mathematical vocabulary as you ask, 'Does this one hold more/less than this one?'. 'Which do you think will be the last one?' 'Why?' Once they are in order extend the activity by encouraging the children to put the numeral cards on in the right order, one to ten. The next time, mix the bottle order again and see if they can order them from the least to the most full. At first the children will need adult support to do this but eventually they should be able to do it without much help. Another time vary the size and shape of the bottles. Talk about which one they think holds the most. Test using a jug to see if their predictions are correct. For variation, repeat the song using different coloured water, big bottles, small bottles, and so on.

The water tray

It is useful to display some key questions, words and phrases on the wall near the water tray:

Which holds the most?

How many cupfuls to fill the bottle?

Which holds the least?

What happens when you pour some water out?

How many spoonfuls do you think it will take to fill the egg cup?

Does it float?

empty	full
more than	less than
holds	pour
fill	cupful
spoonful	under
float	

Incidental learning will also take place during spontaneous water play. Children will learn about the properties of shape as they use the tall and narrow containers compared with small wide bottles. They will discover that pouring out of a round-topped container such as a jug is easier than pouring out of a margarine carton. They will use mathematical language as they play co-operatively together. 'You hold this and I'll fill it up to the top'. They will estimate how much water is needed to fill the containers and find out if they over-estimated when it overflows. You can encourage this type of prediction with questions which make the children think about what is happening. 'How many cupfuls do you

think you will need to fill this bottle with water?' 'Shall we see if you are right?' They will also discover that there will be some 'left over' and an exact number of cups may not fill the jug.

Floating and sinking

A popular activity in any 'Water' topic is floating and sinking. This can be extended to develop sorting skills. Always encourage children to predict the outcome and explain the reasons for their prediction. The aim is to help children decide whether the object belongs in a set of 'things that float' or 'things that do not float'. Objects might include:

wooden spoon

metal spoon

plastic spoon

stone

piece of wood

cork

feather

set of keys

When they find out which float and which sink, the one set could be put in one bucket of water, the other in another. Let the children handle the objects and put them into the right set. Commercially produced plastic or foam numbers and sponge shapes can be added for extra fun.

Water play in general and playing with various boats will encourage the use of positional language:

On top of the water

Under the water

Along the water

Through the water

Over the bridge

Under the bridge

Assessment
❏ Does the child play voluntarily in the water?

❏ Does the child use language such as 'full' and 'empty'?

❏ Can the child identify which container holds the most?

❏ Can the child predict how much water is needed to fill a container?

❏ Can the child pour water from a jug to a cup without spilling too much?

In boat play children could build bridges for boats to pass under. They could learn about distance as they watch how far the boats sail. 'What happens when you put a passenger on the boat?' Boats and plastic buckets can be ordered by size or sorted by colour. Other ideas include setting up games such as 'Hook the duck' or magnetic fishing where each plastic duck/fish has a numeral on. The children fish out the ducks and if they recognise the numeral they say the number name. Older children could score by adding small numbers together or using a tally chart.

Washing

Children really enjoy washing up! Provide various things each day to be washed. If they had all the cups and saucers, for example, they could then match them one to one as they put them back on the table. Similarly if they wash the knives, forks and spoons. Provide a drainer and a cutlery tray so children have to sort out where to put things. With the teapot and saucepans they would have to match the lids according to size. Another time they could wash all the dolls' clothes and when they are dry sort and match as they redress the dolls.

Which button?

Colour recognition is an important part of learning to sort and classify. Once a child can sort by colour you know that he is beginning to recognise similarities and differences. If they can match colour, then they can move on to matching more complex arrangements, such as shapes.

Sorting and matching colour is, at the early stage, probably more important than naming colours. Activities to encourage sorting and matching colours should be practical, with the adult reinforcing the colour name. Start with two easily distinguishable colours such as red and blue and use everyday objects such as plates, buttons, socks or toy cars.

First, find out if the children already know the colour names. Hold up a red object and ask, 'What colour do you think this is?' If someone gives the right answer, repeat back to the rest of the children, 'Yes, it's red isn't it?' 'Can anyone else find another red (button)?'

Ask the children to pick out all the red buttons and put them into a pot. Repeat the activity until they can sort the red from the blue on their own. Say something like 'Now here are some buttons. I want you to sort them out into two colours. This colour (show colour) in this pot and this colour in the other.' Observe the children and record their achievements. Take out one of the colours and introduce a new colour so you have, for example, red and green instead of red and yellow. Gradually increase the number of

colours to be sorted until all the primary colours are included.

Of course, this type of activity alone will not be enough to help children recognise and name colours. Some children have difficulty remembering the colour names and this needs to be encouraged in as many ways as possible. At first, they will recall colours which have some meaning to them, such as the colour of their favourite

jumper or the colour of their car.

Colour recognition needs to be reinforced in the daily routine and in other learning areas. A colour table and a 'colour of the week' will draw children's attention to the colour and help them practise. (For more ideas, see other titles in this series, particularly *What Learning Looks Like: Science and Technology*.) If the colour of the week is red you could organise some of the following activities:

❑ children contribute to a collection of red objects on the colour table;

❑ background display of red paintings and pictures of red things, for example fire engines;

❑ red cotton reel printing (red on a white background);

❑ red felt-tips or crayons on the drawing table or easel;

❑ colour the water, sand and playdough with red food colouring;

❑ bake red cakes (or decorate with red icing);

❑ display red flowers on the colour table;

❑ provide red apples at snack time;

❑ choose children wearing red to line up first;

❑ hold a red day when all the staff and children wear something red;

❏ dyeing handkerchiefs red;

❏ bubble painting red;

❏ hang a row of red socks on the washing line.

Once you are sure the children know the primary colours, expand the focus to other colours such as purple, black, brown and white.

It is important for children to learn about colours in a concrete not abstract way. Draw their attention to colours in nature such as fruit, animals and plants. Use the environment to illustrate the various shades and tones. Allow children to explore colour at the easel. How often do you have black or grey paint available? Activities and discussion could also be planned around themes such as light and dark or black and white.

Colour activities can also incorporate pattern making and recognition (see pages 22-23). Asking the children to print a pattern using red and blue would also reinforce the activity of sorting red and blue buttons.

Other aspects of the mathematical Early Learning Goals can be reinforced using colour as a stimulus. Children could count numbers of red and blue then work out how many altogether. They could make patterns relating to colour using coloured wooden or plastic bricks. Draw children's attention to colours as they play with peg boards, Unifix cubes and make necklaces by threading beads. Symmetrical colour patterns can be made using cubes, peg boards or by threading beads. Other useful resources include colour spinners (which children could make themselves), dice with coloured spots and commercial colour matching games. Older children could record their favourite colours on a class bar chart.

Extend into role play

Set up the role-play area as a decorator's store or an artist's shop. As well as all the opportunities for maths through role play (see pages 36-39) this will involve sorting the paint tins or pots by colour, shape and size; organising paintbrushes into pots. The shop would sell crayons sorted into wax and pencil crayons, also sorted by colour. Children would need to select short and long handled paintbrushes for customers. Ask your local store for an old wallpaper book for children to look at the colours and patterns. Display paint charts and copies or posters of artists' paintings for children to talk about.

Alternatively, set up the area as a haberdashery. You would need different coloured wools and cottons; various coloured ribbons and fabrics with varying colours and patterns; pots for various coloured buttons.

Monitor and assess

Failure to name colours is often seen as a signal that a child has cognitive difficulties. However, it is the recognition which is important. If the child can sort and match colours he may simply not have reached the stage of retaining the colour names. Nevertheless, if in spite of all your best efforts, most children in your group have managed to sort, match and recognise primary colours but there is one child who simply seems to have a mental block, this may be a cause for concern and will need monitoring. Is the child colour blind? On the one hand it is important not to judge a child as 'low ability' simply because he does not know his colours. On the other hand, an inability to sort, match or recognise any colours at all indicates the need to monitor and assess the child's learning across the curriculum.

Early Learning Goals

❏ Count reliably up to ten everyday objects.

❏ In practical activities and discussion begin to use the vocabulary involved in adding and subtracting.

❏ Talk about, recognise and recreate simple patterns.

❏ Use language such as 'circle' or 'bigger' to describe the shape and size of solid and flat shapes.

All about me

Body language

This theme can be adapted to incorporate various mathematical elements including counting, recognising numerals and using the language of comparison. Most children like to talk about themselves and their families and it is important to capitalise on their ideas and experiences which will form a large part of the topic. Topics arising linked with this theme will vary from group to group but there are a few common areas which make good starting points for discussion and planned activities.

My body

You will need:

Child size cut-out picture of body

Detachable numeral cards 1-10

A good starting point is talking about their bodies. Sing the action rhyme 'Head, shoulders, knees and toes', then take each body part in the song and ask 'How many?' This will bring:

one head

two shoulders

two knees

ten toes

Early Learning Goals

❏ Say and use number names in order in familiar contexts.

❏ Count reliably up to ten everyday objects.

❏ Recognise numerals 1 to 9.

two eyes

two ears

one mouth

one nose

Use the child size large cut-out template of a child and draw a line with an arrow pointing from the body parts to the side of the picture. Explain to the children that you are going to look at the numbers which match your body picture. Then choose one child at a time to match the numeral to the body part in the action rhyme. You can

extend this to include the other body parts - arms, hands, fingers, elbows, feet. Obviously the number two will feature heavily in any discussion.

Two eyes

Two legs

Two ears

Two shoulders

Two knees

Two arms

Two hands

one..two...three..four..five!

Introduce children to the idea of a pair - of gloves, shoes, socks - because we need two the same. Older children could investigate symmetry. 'Tommy Thumb' is another popular rhyme for comparing the size of fingers.

A good alternative for older children is a skeleton where you can extend the idea further and talk about how many bones in our legs and how many ribs. Some may even be introduced to numbers of internal organs - how many lungs? In their play children will enjoy looking at themselves in mirrors and talking about their body parts. They could draw or paint a self-portrait of their face using a mirror. Do they have the correct number of eyes and ears?

Go on to look at and compare the individual characteristics of the children. Measure each child and mark their name on the height chart. Talk about who is the tallest, who is taller than who and so on. Ask individual children, 'Are you taller than Sam?' The same could be done with weight. 'Who is heavier than Mrs Jones?'

Explain how numbers are used to represent the sizes of clothes, for example shoes. Use old shoes to do printing then match the pairs or match the shoe shape, size and tread pattern to the print. Use stories and songs about size such as 'Goldilocks and the three bears' to reinforce the mathematical language. Sort and count how many children have blue eyes, brown eyes, black hair, long hair, short hair and so on, recording, for example, using tally charts or pictures from magazines.

My family

Another good stimulus for talking about numbers is to explore photographs of the children's houses and families. In small group discussion, ask key questions such as:

❑ How many brothers do you have?

❑ How many sisters?

❑ How many people in your family altogether?

❑ How many animals do you have?

❑ How old are you?

❑ How old is your brother?

❑ How old do you think your mum is?

❑ Who is the oldest?

❑ Who is the tallest?

❑ How many bedrooms are there in your house?

❑ What is your house number?

❑ How many people are in your photograph?

❑ How many windows can you see on the front of your house?

Children can draw pictures of their families. Write captions underneath: 'Here is mummy. She is 21' or 'There are 4 people in my family'. Older children could make an ongoing book about their family. These activities will help children recognise that a numeral represents the total number in a set.

What did I do yesterday?

Children could discuss and draw pictures to illustrate their daily routine or experiences. Younger children could just talk and draw about before and after lunchtime - 'In the morning' and 'In the afternoon'. This will introduce sequencing and early ideas about time.

Language such as 'yesterday', 'today' and 'tomorrow' is often confusing for young children. Make each child a little book with three pages. Get them to talk and draw about something they do each day for three days. On the first day talk about today. On the second day talk about today, yesterday and tomorrow. On the third day talk about yesterday (and the day before).

You could also use the days of the week here: 'On Mondays we go swimming'; 'On Tuesdays I go to ballet'. Older children could keep a diary of a week. They could use emergent writing or the adult could write in the information and the children draw the pictures.

The clothes shop

Organise the role-play area as a clothes shop. Children will be able to measure each other with tape measures. Provide mirrors for them to look in and judge whether the dress, hats or trousers are too big, too small, too long or too short. Provide dressing-up clothes of various sizes including items that would fit older children, babies and adults. Encourage older children to think about the idea of 'medium' or 'average' size as a middle point between the extremes.

Assessment

❑ Does the child know her age?

❑ Can she say how many brothers/sisters she has?

❑ Can the child identify a 'pair', for example of shoes?

❑ Does the child attempt to record numbers during role play?

People who help us

Equipment and uniforms

This theme crosses all six areas of learning in the English Early Learning Goals. It is strongly associated with Knowledge and Understanding of the World and Communication, Language and Literacy. However, with careful planning Mathematical Development can also be fostered. Of course, much depends on which people you decide to focus on. Many settings plan to concentrate on one person or occupation each week as the main springboard for children's experiences, covering as many as six different mini-topics in half a term.

Planning should focus on those people who are closest to the children's own experiences and this will vary according to the location of your group and the type of community it serves. A nursery in a rural farming area consisting of small village communities may choose people such as:

The farmer	The milkman
The postman	The vet
The bus driver	The doctor

You might also want to introduce one or two less familiar occupations. An inner-city group may well include some of the above but could draw on local resources such as:

Fire station	Police station
Hospital	Travel agents
Supermarket	Railway station
Fast food outlet	

You may also wish to compare occupations in the town and the country and include, for example a farmer. All these people help everyone but children have less regular contact with certain people than others.

Starting points

The starting points for this topic are small and large group discussion, looking at artefacts, videos, pictures, and books as well as visits by the people or visits to the settings where the people work. You could begin by asking the children if they know what jobs their parents do. Another enjoyable activity is matching clothes, equipment or hats to occupations. Ask 'Who does this belong to?'

Doctors and nurses

When looking at books or posters ask the children to count how many doctors they can see, how many nurses, how many patients, and so on. Draw attention to the patterns on the nurses uniforms. Looking closely at equipment used by doctors and nurses offers excellent opportunities to 'count reliably up to ten using everyday objects', 'recognise numerals 1 to 9' and 'say and use number names in familiar contexts'.

Equipment

A whole range of medical equipment involves recognising numerals, using number names, measurement and counting. A stopwatch could form the focus of a group discussion and you could say the number names as you take the children's pulses . You may be able to borrow a manual heart monitor or you could make a model one. Children could listen to each others' heartbeats and count steadily. Blood pressure gauges - either toy or real ones purchased from chemists - also help children in recognising and using numbers in practical situations.

making a fever scan (small group activity)

You will need:

Strips of paper or flexible card

Felt tips

Number line or chart (to refer to)

Fever scan

Show the group a head fever scan and a normal thermometer. See if anyone knows what they are for. Talk about hot and cold. The higher the

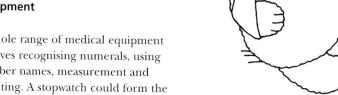

Early Learning Goals

❑ Count reliably up to ten everyday objects.

❑ Recognise numerals 1 to 9.

❑ Use developing mathematical ideas and methods to solve practical problems.

number on the thermometers, the hotter the patient is. Let the children look closely and see if they recognise any of the numerals. Take turns at taking each others' temperatures and looking at the numbers. Then explain that you are going to make your own fever scans for the role-play hospital. Give each child a strip of paper and show them how to divide it, by drawing lines with the felt-tip. Younger ones may need support with this. You could draw the lines in with a pencil and get the children to draw over the top with the felt-tip pen. You could write the numerals or let the children use their own emergent symbols and codes for numerals. Alternatively you could use self-adhesive dots. Children can then role play taking each others' temperature, taking the dolls' temperature and more than likely they will all take yours with their own fever scans. Adults could encourage children to 'find one more or one less' as they join in children's play, asking 'My temperature has gone up. It was six before and now it's one more. How many degrees is it now?'

Hospital role play

Involve the children in designing the area. Ask, 'How many beds will we need?' 'How many blankets?' If it is a surgery some chairs could represent the waiting room where there could also be a clock and some posters. Create a receptionist area behind a table with a telephone, telephone directory, pen and diary or

appointments book. These activities will encourage children to use the language of time and dates. The consulting room will need scales, doctor's kits, height chart and a pad to write prescriptions or make notes on the patient.

Children will use their developing mathematical ideas and methods to solve simple problems as they experiment with bandages of various lengths to wrap around each other or the dolls. They will match the sizes of the dolls to the beds. They will be problem-solving as they tuck the patients into bed with different size/shape sheets and blankets. Other useful role-play resources include:

> bathroom scales; tape measures; height and weight charts; stethoscope; boxes (as beds); dolls (various sizes); blood pressure gauge; stopwatches; fever scans; assorted bandages/slings.

You could also turn the dolls' house into a hospital and collect small world figures of doctors and nurses.

Count the spots

You will need:

Simple, clearly drawn symmetrical faces

Self-adhesive, red circles

This is rather an abstract activity but older children will enjoy it. Draw a line down the centre of the face so it is divided into symmetrical halves. Ask the children to stick some red self-adhesive spots on the face. They could then count the spots they have put on each side. Introduce counting and the vocabulary of simple addition, for example:

> 'You've got four spots. Put another one here. Now how many spots are there?'

> 'Whose face has the most spots?'

Assessment

❑ Does the child use numbers in role play?

❑ Does the child recognise numerals on equipment, such as calculators and telephones?

❑ Can the child count to the rhythm of a timer?

❑ Does the child attempt to record numbers during role play?

'How many spots on this side?'

'How many on this side?'

'How many altogether?'

Fire-fighters

Contact your local fire station to see if they will send a fire engine out or arrange a visit. Look carefully at the firefighters' uniform. Count the buttons. Are there any numbers on the helmet? Compare various size helmets. Look at various size ladders (your caretaker or window cleaner may help here). Count the steps. See if the children can estimate which is the longest ladder without counting. Is the ladder wide or narrow?

Build a model fire engine from cardboard for the children to play in. How many fire-fighters will fit in the front or the back? How many windows, doors or wheels will it need? What shape will they be? Use positional language such as 'up' and 'down' the ladder. Look at the fire-fighters' boots and gloves. What size are they? Are they big or small? Are they thick?

Adapt these ideas to fit in with the person you are looking at. Keep the ideas simple and as practical as possible. Although it is important not to force the mathematics into the topic it is just as important not to overlook the potential for Mathematical Development in your topic planning.

Planning for Mathematical Development

These pages explain how the 15 activities in this book cover all the Early Learning Goals for Mathematical Development.

Early Learning Goals for mathematical Development

M1 Say and use number names in order in familiar contexts.

M2 Count reliably up to ten everyday objects.

M3 Recognise numerals 1 to 9.

M4 Use developing mathematical ideas and methods to solve practical problems.

M5 In practical activities and discussion begin to use the vocabulary involved in adding and subtracting.

M6 Use language such as 'more' or 'less' to compare two numbers.

M7 Find one more or one less than a number from 1 to 10.

M8 Begin to relate addition to combining two groups of objects, and subtraction to 'taking away'.

M9 Use language such as 'greater', 'smaller', 'heavier' or 'lighter' to compare quanitities.

M10 Talk about, recognise and recreate simple patterns.

M11 Use language such as 'circle' or 'bigger' to describe the shape and size of solid and flat shapes.

M12 Use everyday words to describe position.

Let's make patterns (pages 22-23)

These activities develop children's ability to talk about, recognise and recreate patterns. They help children to notice patterns in the environment and look for relationships. They form the early stages of understanding patterns and relationships in number.

Related goal: M10

• • • • • • • • • • • • • • • • • •

Measuring up (pages 24-25)

These activities develop children's use and understanding of mathematical vocabulary, and the language of comparison. This helps children to use mathematics as a powerful tool for communication and to apply their understanding of mathematical concepts such as balance in problem-solving situations.

Related goals: M4, M6, M9, M11

• • • • • • • • • • • • • • • • • •

Getting into shape (pages 26-29)

This theme develops children's abilities to sort, match and compare shapes. It involves using mathematical language to describe flat and solid shapes. It exposes children to shapes in the world about them. The shape week and the shape hunt help children remember the specific properties of individual shapes. Children are encouraged to notice similarities and differences between shapes in a variety of ways.

Related goal: M11

Exploring number (pages 30-31)

A range of activities to help children count reliably for a purpose. Emphasis is placed on the value of interactive displays and number rhymes to practise using number names, counting, addition and subtraction and number recognition. The big book activity develops the idea of ordering numbers in correct sequence.

Related goals M1, M2, M3, M5, M7

• • • • • • • • • • • • • • • • • • • •

Sorting and matching (pages 32-35)

The washing activities develop children's knowledge and understanding of mathematical criteria relating to shape, size and quantity. Sorting the socks encourages language of comparison. The washing basket activity introduces a range of key words in a practical and enjoyable context. The matching activities develop one-to-one correspondence which helps with counting reliably.

Related goals: M2, M4, M9

• • • • • • • • • • • • • • • • • •

Maths through role play (pages 36-39)

Maths through role-play activities, especially shopping, covers most of the Early Learning Goals. Well-planned role play provides a meaningful context for children to use, practise and apply what they know. The role of the adult in the role-play area is to observe, extend and support children's

learning. The shoe shop encourages early ideas about measurement and comparing sizes; the cafe involves counting, matching and one-to-one correspondence. The market stall provides opportunities for counting and sorting for a real purpose.

Related goals M1, M2, M3, M4, M9, M11

● ● ● ● ● ● ● ● ● ● ● ● ● ● ● ● ● ● ●

Your number's up! (pages 40-41)

These activities ensure children have plenty of practice in recognising numerals and in learning to order them. The number line promotes children's ability to distinguish numbers from letters, know number names and read numerals in a variety of contexts

Related goals: M1, M3

● ● ● ● ● ● ● ● ● ● ● ● ● ● ● ● ● ● ●

Promoting mathematical language (pages 42-45)

The obstacle course is a physical activity which helps children to understand and use positional language. It extends Mathematical Development beyond number related goals. It helps children develop the skills and vocabulary tools to solve simple practical problems.

Related goals: M4, M5, M9, M11 and M12

● ● ● ● ● ● ● ● ● ● ● ● ● ● ● ● ● ● ●

Addition and subtraction (pages 46-47)

These activities encourage children to understand the idea of partitioning and combining groups of objects. They introduce the use of vocabulary relating to early addition and subtraction and emphasise the practical nature of finding one more or less than a given number from 1 to 10.

Related goals: M5, M6, M7, M8

● ● ● ● ● ● ● ● ● ● ● ● ● ● ● ● ● ● ●

Problem-solving (pages 48-49)

Gives examples of how children can be encouraged to use the developing mathematical ideas and methods developed throughout this book to solve practical problems.

Related goal: M4

● ● ● ● ● ● ● ● ● ● ● ● ● ● ● ● ● ● ●

Maths for all seasons (pages 50-53)

This theme helps children develop a sense of time and pattern in nature. A number of activities encourage sorting, counting and matching, others introduce ordering and sequencing real objects. Outdoor activities are included in this theme. It is linked with other learning areas.

Related goals: M2, M9, M11

● ● ● ● ● ● ● ● ● ● ● ● ● ● ● ● ● ● ●

Ten green bottles (pages 54-55)

This explains how playing at the water tray is a source of mathematical language and sorting activities. Suggests ideas as to how a topic on water can extend positional vocabulary and help children understand capacity.

Related goals: M3, M4, M9, M12

Which button? (pages 56-57)

Mainly related to number tasks including adding and subtracting, sharing, matching and sorting. There are ideas for reinforcing colour recognition in the daily routine. The role play suggestions provide a meaningful context for sorting.

Related goals M2, M5, M10, M11

● ● ● ● ● ● ● ● ● ● ● ● ● ● ● ● ● ● ●

Body language (pages 58-59)

This theme is adapted to incorporate counting reliably and number recognition as well as using the language of comparison. The activities focus around the body as a resource for mathematical development and experiences.

Related goals: M1, M2, M3

● ● ● ● ● ● ● ● ● ● ● ● ● ● ● ● ● ● ●

Equipment and uniforms (pages 60-61)

The activities suggested encourage children to use and apply their understanding of number in a familiar context. The focus is on using real objects and situations to achieve the goals for Mathematical Development. In particular, the activities encourage the recognition of numerals, counting everyday objects and use of mathematical language as well as sorting and matching skills.

Related goals: M2, M3, M4

● ● ● ● ● ● ● ● ● ● ● ● ● ● ● ● ● ● ●

Planning chart

Mathematical Development	ELG 1	ELG 2	ELG 3	ELG 4	ELG 5	ELG 6	ELG 7	ELG 8	ELG 9	ELG 10	ELG 11	ELG 12
Let's make patterns!										✓		
Measuring up		✓		✓		✓			✓		✓	
Getting into shape		✓									✓	
Exploring number	✓	✓	✓		✓		✓					
Sorting and matching		✓		✓					✓			
Maths through role play	✓	✓	✓	✓					✓		✓	
Your number's up	✓		✓									
Promoting mathematical language				✓	✓				✓		✓	✓
Addition and subtraction				✓	✓	✓	✓					
Problem-solving				✓							✓	
Seasons: Maths for all seasons		✓			✓				✓		✓	
Water: Ten green bottles			✓	✓					✓			✓
Colour: Which button?		✓	✓							✓	✓	
All about me: Body language	✓	✓	✓									
People who help us: Equipment and uniforms			✓	✓								